Write your life stories

THE WORKBOOK

Includes inspiring extracts from published authors, memoir writers and students

by Jo Parfitt

Learn how to add SPICE to your life stories

'Sharing what I know to help others to grow'

Write your life stories

Home study workbook

Includes inspiring extracts from published authors, memoir writers and students

by Jo Parfitt

Learn how to add SPICE to your life stories

First edition March 2010
Revised November 2016

First Published Great Britain 2010
by Summertime Publishing

ISBN 978-1-904881-26-1

Designed by Kim Molyneaux
Edited by Carolyn Vines and Linda March

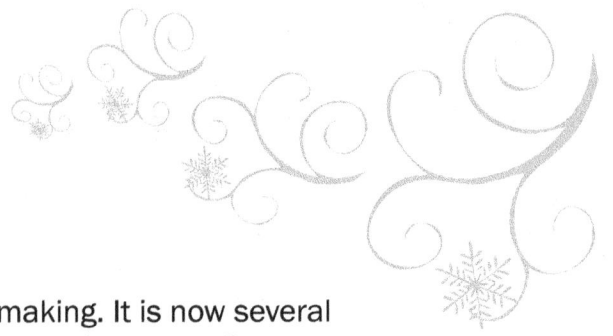

Acknowledgements

This home study program has been a long time in the making. It is now several years since I first decided to turn my popular live workshops into an online course. Two years of brainstorming with friends and colleagues followed, while I read every memoir I could lay my hands on.

I have many people to thank, but firstly and most importantly, I need to thank The Expatriate Archive Centre in The Hague. It was they who encouraged me to create this workshop in order to inspire people to write their life stories and add them to their collection. The archive, its then director Elske van Holk, archivist Rosita Arnts and administrator Katrin Fraenkl were a constant source of support, ideas, material and workspace. The archive generously sponsored the creation of the DVD of my Start Writing Your Life Stories workshop held on their premises in 2009 and booked the talented Jimmy Moya to do that.

I also need to thank Carolyn Vines not only for her meticulous editing but also for being my number one sounding board. Carolyn has patiently given feedback on the variety of permutations this program has taken on its way to its current state.

My family have been more than supportive. My husband Ian, has been with me every step of the way, discussing production, costings and other less creative aspects of this course that, frankly, are not my favourite occupations. He has also taken lessons from my chief sound engineers, our sons Sam and Josh, who have run the recording studio we set up in our home, so that he too can join in the fun at creating and editing the audio files you can now enjoy. My gratitude, of course, goes to Sam and Josh, who have endured an endless stream of visitors coming to record reading their work.

But finally, and no means least, my thanks go to those students who attend my Write Your Life Stories workshops wherever I may go in the world. You are my inspiration. Watching you grow in skill and confidence is a gift I do not take for granted. Many of my students have generously agreed to have their work included in this program, on my website and as bonus tracks. To have their personal work held under the microscope is one thing, but to agree to recite their work too and navigate our dangerous Dutch staircase en route to the studio deserves many thanks. In no particular order, you are: Barbara Reale, Maggie Myklebust, Fanny Bernstein, Debbie Beasley-Suffolk, Celeste Maguire, Melinda Roos, Kim Brice, Carolyn Vines, Adriana Volenikova, Dominique Boulstridge, Trish Huisman, Sandra Forbes, Sue Valentine, Cecilia Götherstrom and Ellen Rosina. Laura Stephens and Sue Ventris, who live in America and Australia respectively, agreed to let me use their work but allowed others to record it.

To those published authors who generously allowed me to include their work in my program, thanks go to Mike Harling, Paul Allen, Peter Gosling, Sheila Bender, Robin Pascoe, Ruth van Reken, Anika Smit, Mahbob Abdullah, Leslie-Ann Bosher, David Sedaris, Maria Yarborough Orhon and Cathy Dobson. Thanks must go to Anastasia Ashman of *Tales from the Expat Harem*, for allowing me to use Maria Yarborough Orhon's extract, to Zodiac Publishing for the extract from *How to be a Global Grandparent* and to the *Expatriate Archive Centre* for allowing

me to include extracts from *The Sourcebook* and *Life on the Move*, two anthologies that are based on their collection.

Thanks to Julia Kohnert, Carolyn Vines, Natasha Forbes, Trish Huisman, Kim Brice and Peter Gosling who agreed to record work from those who could not come to the recording studio.

Jo Parfitt

Every attempt has been made to contact and name everyone who has been involved in this project. If for any reason your name does not appear on this list, then you have my deep apology.

Contents

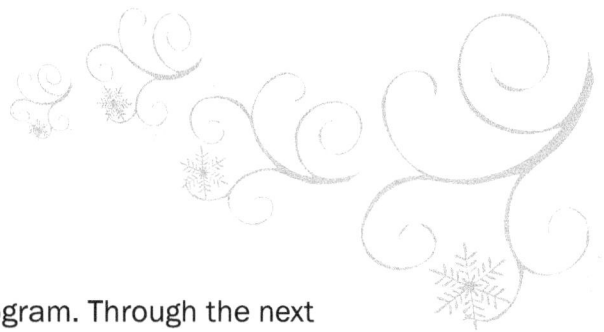

Welcome

Welcome to the **Write Your Life Stories** home study program. Through the next eight lessons, you will be inspired and empowered to start writing your life stories so that they inspire those who read them. Whether you want to write your memoir, keep an effective journal, write a blog or column, preserve your defining moments as a legacy for your grandchildren or simply ensure that your experiences do not go to waste, this program will give you the tools to turn your memories into memoir.

This program will change the way that you think about your life experiences. You will begin to recognise how valuable they are and how they deserve to be preserved. This program will change the way you compose, review and polish your stories so that they can live again each time you, or someone else reads them. Your life is rich and filled with stories that will delight and inspire others. I am here to help you make your writing dreams come true. Along the way you will learn:

- **How to spice up your life stories**
- **The seven steps to writing life stories**
- **The editing process**
- **How to get inspired**
- **Twenty most common mistakes**

Which way?

There are many ways to write life stories. You need to choose your way. This home study program will get you used to writing. It will also introduce you to many methods that will trigger your memories and kick start new ideas. Like the aerobic warm up in an exercise class that you do for the first time, you will find that there are lots of new steps to try. You may feel odd or uncomfortable at first, though ultimately you will feel liberated as your memories emerge from hiding.

Your story

You each have your own stories and each story will deserve a different way of telling it. Try not to judge your writing by the extracts included in this program. There is no value in making comparisons. You have your stories, and they need to be told in a way that is unique to you. Write them using your natural voice, which is the voice you use for letters home or your journal. This is how the real you sounds. Are there some stories that you often find yourself telling over a dinner table? Do some of your life experiences keep coming back to you as they resonate through the years? Are there some defining moments that stay in your mind like snapshots? If so, these are the stories you should share now. They define you and your life. Give these memories a voice.

Course components

All additional course materials can be downloaded from us. You may need a password to access this material.

To receive the link to the materials, please email publisher@summertimepublishing.com with Coursework as the subject of the email.

If you would prefer to receive physical versions of the materials, please ask. These can be provided at extra cost.

This course comprises the following:

Workbook

This **workbook** is the main tool for this course. Everything you need is here. You will either have received this workbook as a download file, or in print form. If you work through it on the screen, and are online, then you have the ability to click through to the many hyperlinks to find out more about the writers who are featured. You will also be able to access the audio files directly.

Video

A **video** of a 60-minute Start Writing Your Life Stories workshop, held at the Expatriate Archive Centre in The Hague. You can download and watch it on your device. It is advised that you watch this first.

Podcasts

Eight **podcasts**, one for each lesson. Each podcast provides an audio version of the lesson so that you can reinforce the lesson and listen to the extracts whenever you wish. They have been read, when possible, by their original authors. You can take the lessons in any order, but it is advised that you take LESSONS ONE and TWO before moving on to the others.

Bonus lesson - The editing process

By the time you reach the end of this program, you will be ready to start editing your work yourself. Our **bonus lesson** will help you do that. With a list of the 20 most common mistakes as a reference, watch a piece of writing move through the editing process. Follow its progress through five edits as it is polished, returned to the student, improved and returned again until it is ready.

Bonus inspiration - stuck for ideas? Not now!

After you have completed the course, you can download more than **200 Just Write inspirational stickers**. Each sticker shows a word or phrase that has been designed to trigger your memory and inspire you to write a piece of life story.

How do you use the inspirational stickers?

Paste a sticker in a notebook and start writing your story. Or try selecting some words from any sticker as the title for a piece that you complete on your computer. Whenever you write, write freely until you have no more to say. Write yourself dry.

Just Write inspirational stickers come to you as a PDF file, formatted to print on a sheet of twelve standard labels. Print the file directly onto these labels or onto sheets of A4 paper that you cut up into rectangles and stick into your notebook as you need them.

Getting inspired

Whenever I'm stuck for ideas, I find nothing more inspiring than reading the work of those who have written their life stories and books by professional writers. That's why, at the very end of this program, you will find a reading list that will help you **get inspired**.

You will need

A notebook

Treat yourself to a beautiful notebook that you will use to write down all your ideas and stories.

Use the front section of the book, working forwards, to write your stories or drafts of stories. Use the back section of the book, working backwards, to note your ideas for stories, or the memories or ideas or insights that come to you as you work through the course.

Technology - computer, Word and email

If you are following the program and have purchased the **Personal Feedback Program,** you will need to submit your completed tasks by email to jo@joparfitt.com. Each piece will be marked and edited in Word using the Track Changes and Comments features. It is important that your computer has the Word program and that you submit your homework in this format.

Turnaround time for personal feedback

If you have chosen to follow the **Personal Feedback Program,** then your critiqued homework will be returned to you within two weeks of receipt whenever possible. If a delay is likely owing to problems or holidays, you will be informed.

Feedback will be given only on the first 1,000 words of each homework submitted.

Want to opt for personal feedback on specific exercises?

If you have not already purchased the critique for all eight lessons then you can alternatively have **personal feedback** on specific exercises only, then you may do so. This is charged at £45 per piece to a maximum of 1000 words. To do this, please submit your homework using the naming convention YOURNAMELESSONNUMBER (JANESMITHONE) and pay £45 in advance via Paypal to publisher@summertimepublishing.com. Include the title of the document you are submitting for critique in the payment comments.

Program breakdown

This home study program is divided into eight lessons plus one bonus lesson

- Lesson one – Introduction
- Lesson two – Letting it flow
- Lesson three – Writing about childhood
- Lesson four – A sense of place
- Lesson five – Writing about people
- Lesson six – Writing in themes
- Lesson seven – Writing humour
- Lesson eight – Writing in stories
- BONUS LESSON – The editing process

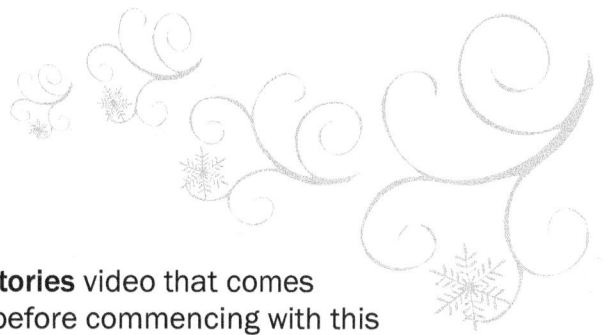

Lesson One – *Introduction*

Your first lesson builds on the **Start Writing Your Life Stories** video that comes with this program. Set aside 40 minutes to watch this before commencing with this lesson. In this lesson you will learn how to **spice up your life stories** as well as the **seven steps to writing life stories**. Then, you put this into practice and compile your first piece of homework.

Lesson Two – *Letting it flow*

Your second lesson will give you the tools that will awaken your creativity and show you how to get ideas.

Lesson Three – *Writing about childhood*

Your third lesson will take you back to when you were a child. Here we will explore the stories from your past and show you how to write about things that happened a long time ago, even if you may have forgotten the details.

Lesson Four – *A sense of place*

Your fourth lesson will focus on setting the scene and describing the places in which your stories take place. The reader needs to feel as if he is there with you and can see, smell, hear, taste and sense all the things you experienced at the time.

Lesson Five – *Writing about people*

Without people your stories can appear a little flat. This lesson will show you how to describe the characters in your stories and make them real. It will teach you how to write about yourself and other people and how to make those characters talk, move and act in an authentic way.

Lesson Six – *Writing in themes*

Sometimes you won't have a specific story to tell, but you will recognise the importance of certain themes in your life. Things like adventure or loss for example, or maybe how your passion for music or travel has dominated your life? This lesson will show you how to bring several smaller incidents together on one theme and turn them into a compelling piece of writing.

Lesson Seven – *Writing humour*

Telling a funny story from your life to friends when you are in the pub or at a dinner party may result in everyone laughing uproariously. Putting the same story down on paper is much harder. This lesson will show you how to make your funny stories just as humorous when you write them down.

Lesson Eight – Writing in stories

It is always a joy to be able to recount a story from your life that feels complete. It has a beginning, middle and an end and, importantly, it resonates with the reader. This lesson will show you how.

Bonus Lesson – The editing process

Once you have completed the course and have practised adding **spice** to your work and following the **seven steps to writing life stories**, you are ready to learn how to improve your work still further. It is time for you to understand **the editing process** and the **twenty most common mistakes** students tend to make and try to avoid them in your own work.

Beyond the program

Once you are inspired and familiar with the way to write compelling life stories, the **getting inspired** resources section and the **Just Write inspirational stickers** will provide you with hours of future ideas.

Want to take your writing further?

We are delighted to offer four more options:

1. Work with us to plan, write, edit and publish your memoir or non-fiction book.

2. Follow our Definite Articles http://www.summertimepublishing.com/definite-articles.html home study program and learn to write and sell articles based on what you know.

3. Follow our Release the Book Within http://www.summertimepublishing.com/release-the-book-within.html home study program and learn how to plan and write your non-fiction book.

4. Start a Writers' Circle and download our free factsheet here http://www.summertimepublishing.com/free-writers-tools.html.

Good luck.

Jo Parfitt

LESSON ONE

Introduction

Welcome to the Write Your Life Stories home study program. During the next eight lessons, you will master the craft of writing compelling life stories. These stories are the events or defining moments in your life that have made you who you are, formed your character and will inspire those who read them.

Do you want to write a better journal? Would you like to be able to document the things that happen to you so that they leap off the page, allowing you to relive those moments each time you read them? Or maybe you want to compile your life stories into a memoir that you could leave as a legacy or craft into a publishable book? Whether you want to write non-fiction that uses elements of your life to inspire others, or whether you want to write a blog, newsletter, column, personal essays or articles, this program will help you write authentically and effectively about your life.

Before we start, we have some groundwork to do. So let me introduce you right away to the tools that will help you write your life stories.

Spice up your life stories

You want your stories to come alive on the page. You want your readers to be able to imagine the scenes, to picture the people and feel what you felt. In other words you need to spice up your writing. In order to help you remember the extra ingredients that will make your writing effective, I have created a simple acronym: SPICE. When you incorporate the five elements of SPICE in your stories your words will leap off the page and allow the reader into your world.

SPICE

- **S**pecifics
- **P**lace
- **I**ncident
- **C**haracter
- **E**motion

Specifics

Adding specific details to your story will bring it to life. If you are writing about a tramp, then saying that he is on Oxford Street in London will conjure up a picture of a busy street, packed with shoppers. Saying that he was outside Buckingham Palace will paint another picture entirely. Put him under the bridge at Embankment and it is different again. Make his cardboard box have Sony stamped on the side, and we imagine it held a television and can visualise the size of it. He could wear a pink fingerless glove on his grimy hand, a Nike sweatshirt or a Wrangler baseball cap. Naming items, brands, landmarks and places adds a new dimension to your story. Naming plants, trees and food, for example, is effective too.

Rather than describing the forest as 'tropical', say it was filled with banana trees, skinny coconut palms and squat, spiky pineapple plants. Instead of saying the view was 'breathtaking', tell us what you see. Naked branches of vast chestnut trees silhouetted against the January mist, maybe? Yellow daffodils, pink and white striped tulips and china blue hyacinths in your flowerbed rather than 'spring flowers'.

Foreign words are useful as they add atmosphere. Put foreign words in italics. In the Hemingway piece in the DVD you just watched, Hemingway writes of the Closerie des Lilas and Boulevard Montparnasse. These street names immediately evoke Paris. He also writes of the plat du jour in such a way that we know he means something on the menu even if we do not speak good enough French to know it means 'dish of the day'.

Give your characters names and labels. If you need to tell us about a school friend, don't call him simply 'my school friend'. Give him a name and help us to understand a little more about him. Maybe he becomes a maths teacher, or is a farmer's son, so say so.

Place

Adding specific details to your stories will help you set the scene. Mentioning palm trees, sand dunes and mosques places us in the Middle East. Your story took place somewhere and that somewhere may be a place with which your readers are not familiar. Set the scene to allow your readers to feel that they are there with you. Show them what you saw. Let them feel the heat of the 100 per cent humidity and how it drenched your clean shirt in seconds. Let them hear the lilting call to prayer from the top of the minaret of the mosque with the onion-shaped dome. Let them bite into the warm Arabic flatbread.

This is what I call 'painting a picture with your pen'. Setting the scene effectively will do just that.

Incident

The best stories are those in which something happens. Perhaps there is a crisis that is overcome, or an amazing coincidence, an accident, an act of kindness or something or someone lost. Telling a story about your grandfather, for example, will be made more interesting if you include a story from his life. Add incident to your stories. Make something happen.

Character

A piece of life story comes alive when you put a person into the story. If your story happens in London, you can describe the buildings, the scenery, the red buses and the black cabs. If you add a person to the story, it can take on an extra dimension. So write about the skinny bus driver who was eating a beefburger while driving you round Trafalgar Square. Tell us about the tramp you saw. Describe how he was arranging sheets of cardboard round his body in the doorway just before settling down for an afternoon nap.

People can be characterised by the things they do and say, the way they move and by their habits or quirks. Even the clothes they wear can be indicative of character, so include these details.

The people in your stories can interact with you, with each other or with the scene. When people interact, they talk. Dialogue makes your stories come to life. It's not always easy to remember what someone really said, so just ensure the dialogue is plausible.

Adding action and character to dialogue

A long sentence can be broken up with action, characterisation and words such as 'she continued'.

Mercedes comes from Spain but has lived in England since she was about six. This is how you could describe her:

> "I still feel Spanish," Mercedes said. "I hate the long, dark winters and crave garlic in my food. What's more, I simply love to dance." She pulled up the polo neck of her fuchsia pink jumper so that it covered her neck and chin and shivered. "Don't get me wrong," she continued, "England is great. I love the beer! But, my heart has always belonged to Marbella."

Imagine that a tramp living in a cardboard box spoke to you. You could characterise him like this:

> "Hey, Mister, have you got a few coins for a cuppa?" he said, peering over the cardboard for a moment and extending a hand that was black with grime.

In this sentence about the tramp, the dialogue is followed by action. He peers over the cardboard and holds out his hand. Action is also used to characterise him. His hand was black with grime. This action gives the story a bit of life.

Using dialogue allows you to show the reader what happened, rather than tell him about it. Rather than writing: 'Jane was angry', show her anger. Have her slamming a door or smashing a plate.

Rather than telling us what someone said to you in reported speech, show us the dialogue. For example:

Bob told me he loved playing the piano more than anything else in the whole wide world.

Becomes

"I love playing the piano more than anything else in the whole wide world," said Bob, stroking the keys with his gentle fingers.

Show us what your characters said. Add the movements they made and show the reactions of other people too. This will bring the scene to life.

If you have opted to take this program with the **Personal Feedback** option, then you will receive personal advice on how to handle dialogue from your tutor.

Emotion

Life story writing is about real things that happen to real people. The reader wants to be there with you, seeing what you saw, feeling what you felt and so on. Be honest about what you felt. Inject authenticity into your writing by sharing your emotions.

The best writing comes from a place of heightened emotion, so don't be shy about being truthful about the way your heart burst with joy when your child was born or split with sorrow when you had to wave goodbye.

And while you should include your own feelings in your writing, remember to include the feelings of the characters in your stories too.

A good way to let the reader understand your feelings is by using a metaphor, simile or other figure of speech. Perhaps you were so happy to be alone that you felt as free and filled with excitement as a butterfly that finds a field full of buttercups?

The best life stories will resonate with the reader and make him nod his head with recognition.

From now on

As you go through this home study program, add SPICE to your stories, spotting its five elements as you listen to the extracts I have chosen. The more you notice these elements in the writing of others, the more natural it will become for you to use them in your own stories. On the following page you will find a chart you can complete each time you are preparing for a story. Feel free to print this as often as you like for your own use.

Want extra copies of the SPICE CHART, on the next page?

You can download extra copies of the SPICE CHART and reprint it as often as you like by emailing publisher@summertimepublishing.com and asking for the PDF.

The SPICE CHART

Specifics

Name some details: the name of the town, the street, the building. The brands you ate/saw/used. The type of car, the names of the flowers and so on.

Place

Where were you? Set the scene. What could you see, hear, taste and so on?

Incident

What happened? What was the sequence of events? The plot?

Character

Who was with you? What did the people with you look like? How did they behave? Did they have a quirk or habit? What did you say to each other? What movement did you or they make while speaking? Maybe you put down a coffee cup, slammed a door, folded your arms or pulled a face?

Emotion

How did the event make you feel? How did the event make the people with you feel?

The seven steps to writing life stories

Few people can produce a perfect first draft. Most work goes through several stages, edits and rewrites. There are seven steps to writing a quality piece of work. I call these the **seven steps to writing life stories**. Following these steps in order will help you create your best work. They are:

1. Compose
2. Review
3. Draft
4. Review
5. Polish
6. Revisit
7. Save

Step One – Compose

The first step to writing a piece of life story is **compose**.

Take your memory, thought, story or idea and think about it for a while. Make a few notes. Complete the SPICE sheets if they help you. You don't need to write in full sentences, just make notes, inspired by my list above.

Step Two – Review

The second step to writing a piece of life story is **review**.

After you have made some notes, but before you start to write your story properly, discuss your idea with someone else. Find someone you trust and ask him or her to listen to your idea. When you have finished, ask your friend to comment on the following:

- The things he or she liked about your idea
- The things he or she wanted to know more about – the scene, how someone looked, what they wore, the weather, how you felt and so on

If it is impossible for you to discuss your idea with someone else, then leave your notebook behind for a few minutes and do something else. You may find it helpful to go for a walk, do the shopping or washing up, for example. While you are doing this, your ideas will start to consolidate and you will start asking yourself questions and thinking of improvements.
Now that you have **composed** your idea and **reviewed** it, you are ready to do your first **draft**.

Step Three – Draft

Now write your piece. This is a first **draft**. It is not going to be perfect. You are not going to agonise over every word. You are just going to write it – from beginning to end. You are not going to keep looking back and revising your work, you are just going to get it down. Write in your natural voice, the way you would speak. If you write fast, you can avoid the inner critic who

is going to do his hardest to put you off track. Do not stop until you have written everything down. Write yourself dry.

Step Four – *Review*

When you have a first draft, congratulate yourself. You did it. You got to the end. You completed a piece of writing. It may not be perfect, but it is done.

It is time to review your work, to find out which bits worked and which bits could do with improvement. The best way to REVIEW your work is with a friend; again, sharing your idea is beneficial. You will find that when you read a piece aloud to yourself, you notice mistakes, but when you read to a third party, those errors scream in your ear. This is way more effective than simply reading your work silently to yourself.

Ask yourself: Did I include SPICE?

- **S**pecifics
- **P**lace
- **I**ncident
- **C**haracter
- **E**motion

Step Five – *Polish*

Your story has been composed, reviewed, drafted and reviewed again. Now you are ready to POLISH it. This is when you make improvements and ensure that you have remembered to include SPICE.

This time you are allowed to go slowly and to take your time, thinking about every word.

Step Six – *Revisit*

If you can, put your edited work to one side for a few days before you look at it again. REVISIT your piece with fresh eyes. Read it aloud again, make any more changes and then, when you are satisfied, your story is complete.

Step Seven – *Save*

Now save your document, print a copy and add it to your folder of finished work. Always remember to take regular back ups. If you are taking the **Personal Feedback Program**, then name your file according to the convention **your name** and then the **lesson number**, such as **tombrownthree** for example.

Putting it into practice

Now let's put all this into practice using a limbering up exercise. You will find a Limbering Up exercise in each of your lessons. It has been designed to prepare you for the homework task that comes at the end of the lesson. If you have taken the **Personal Feedback** option then the Task exercises should be sent to your tutor. The limbering up exercises are for you.

Limbering up

Now that you have learned how to SPICE up your stories, it is time for you to put what you have learned into practice.

Being bad

Think of a time when you did something you shouldn't have done or behaved badly. Maybe you pulled a prank at work or school, or maybe you lost or broke something that wasn't yours? Perhaps you did something silly that had an unexpected effect on someone else?

Before you start writing a complete piece of life story, you need to think about what you are going to include. This stage of the writing process is called **composing**.

Answer the follow questions. Take your time. You do not need to write in full sentences. Just jot down what comes into your head.

Spice up your life stories

Specifics

Name some details: the name of the town, the street, the building. The brands you ate/saw/used. The type of car, the names of the flowers and so on.

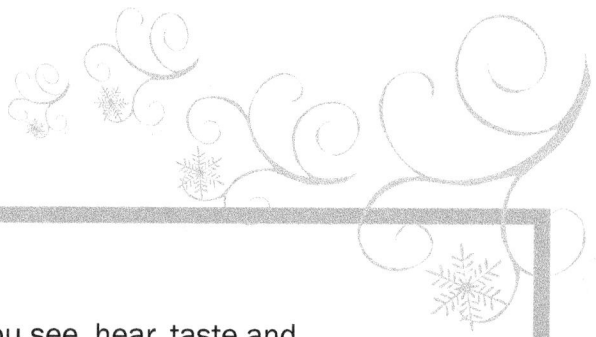

Place

Where were you? Set the scene. What could you see, hear, taste and so on?

Incident

What happened? What was the sequence of events? The plot?

Character

Who was with you? What did the people with you look like? How did they behave? Did they have a quirk or habit? What did you say to each other? What movement did you or they make while speaking? Maybe you put down a coffee cup, slammed a door, folded your arms or pulled a face?

Emotion

How did the event make you feel? How did the event make the people with you feel?

Striped Shirt

This extract from Fanny Bernstein, who is Dutch and whose parents survived Auschwitz, is a powerful piece of writing that leaves us with a sinking heart. The emotion is real. See how she characterises her parents and sets the scene. The dialogue, though spoken in Dutch at the time, has been realistically translated into English.

Until the age of ten, eleven your mother buys your clothes, at least that was how it used to be. Sometimes you may choose yourself something, but in the end it was your mom who decided. As far as I can remember this was how it happened in our family and it never led to any big problems.

My mother had a good taste for fashion, so my sister and I were always nicely dressed. When I look at pictures from when we were kids, I see that sometimes we wore the same dresses, like twins. This, in spite of the fact that I'm five years younger than my sister. But even having to wear the same clothes doesn't bring back unpleasant memories.

When my sister turned 13 or 14 she became more aware of fashion and wanted to choose her own wardrobe. How it happened exactly I don't know, but I do remember very well my parents' reaction when she came home once with her latest acquisition. She entered the room cheerfully with a package nicely wrapped in a beautiful bag of a well-known department store.

"I bought a very nice blouse," she said happily. "You know what, I'm going upstairs to put it on and then I'll show you all how beautiful it is!" and she ran upstairs to her room to put on the new purchase.

Less than five minutes later she entered the room with a radiant smile on her face and dressed in her new purchase. "Well, what do you think?"

"Take it off immediately!" my mother shouted, white as a sheet.

"Why? Don't you like it? Well, I do and I'll keep it on," my sister answered.

"NO," my father said who also looked pale, "you'll immediately take it off and will return it to the shop first thing in the morning."

My sister started to cry softly. "I don't want to return it, I like it very much. I chose this one with my best friend and she liked it too. I'm NOT taking it back," she said stamping her foot.

"You'll damn well return it to the shop!" shouted my mother hysterically. "Not only does it have vertical stripes, which is bad enough, but they're also white and blue like our clothes in the concentration camps. No child of mine will ever wear clothes with blue and white vertical stripes. Understood?"

Making Pasta

Italian Barbara Reale wrote this about a childhood incident that went wrong. To any Italian, making pasta is an everyday occurrence. Even non-Italians can empathise with helping their mother to cook. See how a recent event was the catalyst for a flashback to a childhood memory. It was a sad occasion, but the author finds humour in it.

Last week I hosted a cooking workshop for some Dutch people who wanted to learn what real ravioli looked and tasted like in Italy. They all liked my childish enthusiasm while I was cutting the dough strip with an upside-down glass to form thin and round shaped ravioli. They were having fun and doing their best to trap the stuffing inside the circles of dough when I found myself saying: "No Kim. Wet your fingers first." Two seconds later I realized that these words, that came unfiltered out of my mouth, were the same ones that my mother said to me the first time I was allowed to help her in the kitchen.

I was four and it was the last Christmas I spent with the entire family. It was a melancholic Christmas. My grandfather was going to die and the cold wind of divorce blew back and forth between my parents. I was sitting alone on my grandma's clapped out sofa in her living room, waiting for my cousins to arrive on a visit from where they lived two towns away. The TV was always on loud, even if nobody was watching it. I always thought it was the way my grandma Alide tried to keep her mind off things. I can still see her in her liquorice smelling nightgown revelling in her sadness.

"Nonna, may I help you to lay the table?" I asked.

"No *tesoro*, I am looking for a special cloth to use today."

My mother was in the kitchen preparing ravioli and I decided to go and offer my help even though I already knew she would say no.

"Mamma, may I help you. *Per favore*?" I begged, hopping from one foot to the other.

"No, thanks. Why don't you watch TV?" she said without looking up.

"I don't want to watch TV, I want to learn to cook something."

Unexpectedly my mother handed me a wooden rolling pin and a piece of dough. I felt as excited as someone who had just won a job interview.

Rolling the dough is not an easy task, but I wanted to do my best otherwise I risked losing the job before the exciting part: trapping the stuffing.

Eventually when the dough was thin enough, I was allowed to cut out some circles with an upended wine glass and then to place a small ball of stuffing onto one of them. The sealing part is the most exciting. You have to wet the edges and fold the dough in two, forming a half moon.

My mother watched me during this task, a stern look on her face.

As a child, I knew nothing about this repetitive work, so after a while I heard my mother saying: "Wet your fingers first!"

"Yes Mamma," I replied, but now I wanted to do it my way and I had to do it without my mother's beady eye on me, checking the details.

I spotted a box of dried beans on the low shelf near my knees, so I decided to put a bean in the middle of the ball of stuffing. All I wanted was to express my creativity and surprise my family.

When my cousins arrived, I stopped helping Mamma and ran with them to play outside. When the ravioli were cooked my grandma served them in a brownish roast sauce. We were all enjoying our meal, when my aunt interrupted the holy silence.

"Oh no, there's a raw bean in my ravioli!" she exclaimed.

I forked a raviolo, jumped on the chair and shouted proudly: "It's mine!" I can still see myself as clearly as if it was in a picture, standing on the chair and holding the raviolo high up on my fork. Like a princess with a magic wand I grinned, showing my missing tooth in a face framed by two pigtails. I was surprised. No one was laughing. On the contrary, my aunt was bleeding and everybody looked at me as if I was a murderer. A few seconds later my father was spanking my bottom with a carpet beater. I soon realized that maybe the bean surprise was not such a good idea...

Growing Up

American Maggie Myklebust wrote the following about her childhood summers spent with her sister, Mary Lou, her grandmother, Noney, and great aunt Gaumie. The sense of being naughty is evoked well, as is the scene. We can see the place clearly and imagine we are looking in on the story. See the language she uses. It was just the language of the time.

Finally Monday would come and the weekly routine would begin. Noney would go to work every day, I'm not sure what time she left but she was always home by six. Gaumie's customers would start arriving at nine, therefore we had to be up and our bed turned into a sofa once more. Noney would always leave us each a whole five-dollar bill, to use at the shops on Main Street. With Gaumie busy and before my hard earned curls had a chance to fall, my plan was to be set into action. Dressed in my favorite sundress, doused in perfume, wearing a pair of Noney's perfectly fitting high heel shoes and carrying an ultra chic handbag with my five dollar bill tucked inside, I set out for Main Street, Mary Lou in tow. Then proud as a peacock feeling all grown up I strolled with complete exhilaration down Main Street, the first colonial road in New Jersey. First stop Lopolotte's five and dime shop, which sold all sorts of cheap insignificant things. We, of course, headed for the children's section, which was nothing more than a shelf since the whole store was no bigger than Gaumie's living room. I looked at the paper dolls while Mary Lou rejoiced over finding a paddle with a ball hanging from a rubber string. She explained how she could bounce the ball all day long off the paddle and never have to worry about losing it since it was attached by the rubber string. It always amazed me how she could get so excited over the most trivial of things. Once her purchase was made we headed off to the Jigger Shop for an ice cold Coca-Cola.

On a Monday before lunch, with school being closed for summer it was quiet and empty inside. We didn't mind at all; the August sun was hot and the big paddle fans on the ceiling produced a pleasant breeze. I talked Mary Lou into paying for the sodas because I was saving my five dollars for The Pharmacy. The Pharmacy was one of the few places in Lawrenceville that had air conditioning. In contrast to outside it was freezing cold and astonishingly unpleasant. It felt good when we first stepped in, out of the heat, then after a few minutes we just wanted to run outside and get warm again. Mary Lou looked very puzzled.

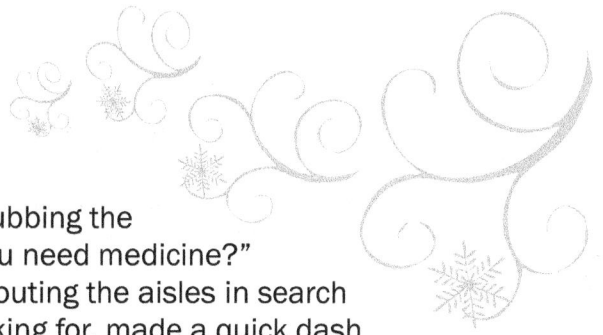

"What are we doing here, Maggie?" she asked, rubbing the goose bumps on her skinny arms. "Are you sick? Do you need medicine?"

My explanation would have to wait; I was busy scouting the aisles in search of something top secret. At last, I found what I was looking for, made a quick dash to the front of the store, paid the cashier and asked for a bag. Outside Mary Lou was dying of a curiosity that could only be put off with a trip to Bentley's grocery store to buy candy. It took her forever to decide and finally settle on some Turkish taffy and a Nestlé's Crunch bar. We raced home as fast as Noney's heels would allow, up the steps into the bathroom where I could change back into an age appropriate outfit. Then into the kitchen for lunch, which was always on the table at twelve sharp. After lunch was when Gaumie really got to work on her sewing since there were rarely any customers in the afternoon.

"Gaumie?" I said to the back of her head as she sat bent over her machine.

"Mmmm," she replied, her mouth full of pins.

"Mary Lou and me, we're just going to cool off in the bathtub, OK?" and without waiting for her reply, we dashed up the steps and locked ourselves in the bathroom, which was where I revealed my secret package. It was a box of Nair hair remover!

"Maggie!" Mary Lou was aghast.

"You can read out the instructions!" I commanded.

I just grinned and soon I was lathering up my legs with the foul smelling cream. I left it on for five minutes as instructed on the box, then began wiping it off with a damp washcloth as Mary Lou watched in complete horror.

"You are in big big trouble!" she repeated. Over and over.

"Mom said I was not allowed to shave my legs. She said nothing about creaming them up." I was triumphant. With that explanation and a promise to spend the rest of the afternoon playing Monopoly with her, my sister was as happy as I was with my nice smooth legs.

Your task

Taking the answers you have noted during the **limbering up** exercise, please write a story of 500-1000 words using the **seven steps for writing life stories** and adding **SPICE**.

Seven steps to writing life stories

1. Compose
2. Review
3. Draft
4. Review
5. Polish
6. Revisit
7. Save

Spice up your life stories

- **S**pecifics
- **P**lace
- **I**ncident
- **C**haracter
- **E**motion

If you are taking the Personal Feedback Program

Please save and name your completed exercise using the YOURNAMEONE naming convention and email it to feedback@joparfitt.com

Your feedback will be returned to you within two weeks.

While you are waiting, feel free to move on to complete **Lesson Two - Letting it flow**. However, wait until you have received your feedback for **Lesson One** before sending off the homework for **Lesson Two**. You will pick up some tips from your tutor that can be used to help you polish your next homework before you send it.

LESSON TWO

Letting it flow

In this second class, learn how to let good ideas come into your mind and how to turn those thoughts into a piece of writing you will be proud of.

Soon you will start to recognise the wealth of stories you have inside you. As you become more aware of these stories and mindful of what triggers your memories, the more ideas you will have.

The next step is to learn how to write the stories that emerge as a result – stories that include SPICE.

- **S**pecifics
- **P**lace
- **I**ncident
- **C**haracter
- **E**motion

As you go through your daily routine, you see things along the way that trigger memories of other things. For example:

- You eat chocolate cake and remember how you helped your mother make it as a child, and that thought leads you to recall your first birthday, when you pushed your chocolate birthday cake onto the floor from your high chair, with the candle still alight on the top.

- You go for a walk and notice the snowdrops, and this takes you back to a time in your childhood, or it makes you remember how your mother too loved snowdrops.

- You eat a biscuit. This could remind you of the biscuits your grandmother used to bake or the times you taught your own children to cook. It does not much matter which direction your mind goes in, but follow it.

It does not matter what it is that you see, or hear, taste or smell or feel that reminds you of something. What matters is that you become inspired to write about something because of it. Your aim is not to produce perfectly crafted stories, but more to learn to write freely and naturally, inspired by a coincidence or something you see. These pieces may not become fully formed stories with developed plot and character. Yet they are valuable, provide insights and increase your confidence as a writer.

This type of random writing is sometimes called free writing, speedwriting or stream of consciousness writing. When these words fall from the pen easily, it is important that you let them come and don't worry about being perfect. The trouble with writing slowly and laboriously, crafting every sentence carefully, is that your inner critic or editor has time to step in and

harass you. This critic has a habit of telling you that what you are writing is no good. Write fast to banish the inner critic and just let the words flow. You will have plenty of time to polish later. Often your best work comes when you forget trying to be perfect but instead focus on getting the words down on paper and reaching the end of your story.

In her book *The Artist's Way*, author, Julia Cameron, proposes that everyone write for ten minutes, first thing in the morning in this way. Writing fairly fast, without stopping to think or taking your pen from the paper is a liberating experience. The constant movement of the pen in your hand somehow seems to stop your inner critic from judging your work. Try it. Let the words flow. Do not worry about what you are writing or where you go with it. Just write.

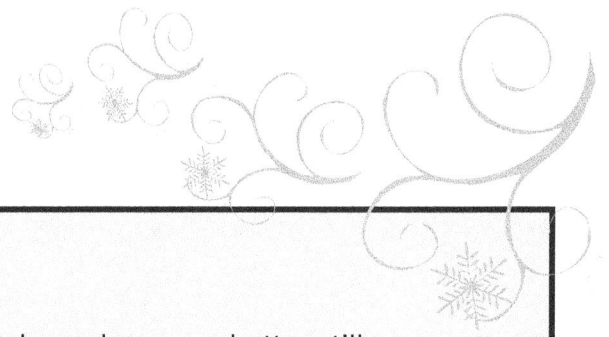

Limbering up

You can complete this exercise in and around your home, or better still you could go out to a café or into the streets or countryside.

1. Look around you, taking in the scene slowly. Walk around the place in which you find yourself, inside and outside. Pay attention. Be inspired by everything you see: the ornaments in the room, the bits and pieces in your bag, on your desk or in the drawer beside your bed. Let your mind wander. A photograph can take you back to another time. Remembering a chance remark can take you on a journey.

2. Now, sit down with a piece of paper and a pen and make a quick note of all the other ideas and thoughts that you had while you were out there, paying attention. Make a list of ideas. If you feel the urge to just write on one of the topics, then do so. Follow your instinct.

3. As soon as you have run out of things to write, your exercise is complete.

The exercise above can be used daily, weekly or just when you have time, as a rich source of ideas. Many established writers do this every day in order to limber up, ready for the real work ahead.

Extracts to inspire you

**Extract – Writing in a New Convertible With The Top Down,
by Christi Killien and Sheila Bender**

Sheila is inspired by the view from her window and her mind wanders to family scenes.

More of Sheila's work can be found at www.writingitreal.com

From my window I see the cherry trees in my backyard. I think about the cycles to watch in a fruit tree – February blossoming, then flower hips growing rounded, deep green foliage in late spring, red cherries against those leaves in summer.

I think of my husband climbing the garage roof, the telephone pole, the ladder and the fence as he forages for food, my son raking cherry leaves in fall, me staring at the eloquence of bare branches in winter, my daughter collecting blossom petals from the lawn each spring.

It doesn't matter that the cherries last only a few weeks – all the rest is fruit too.

Tea

Inspired by the fact that all the students were drinking tea or coffee at our workshops, Debbie Beasley-Suffolk, who is from England, wrote this. Look out for the details she includes about the clothes, tea services and personal features.

I have been a tea-aholic for longer than I can remember. Even before I could reach the pedals on the piano, before my passion for roller skates, and before I decided my boring brown hair had to be dyed another colour – any colour. And so it was; from bombshell blond to racy red, to a disastrous day when the back went a dirty shade of orange and I had to choose between possible suspension from school or the dreaded hairdresser's scissors.

The best ever cup of tea was always to be served at Grandma's. There the whole family was raised in the great British art of Afternoon Tea by a matriarch whose dedication to etiquette belied her working-class roots. She was the family snob, an unwritten title her youngest daughter, my favourite auntie, inherited, who in turn passed the torch to a willing recipient – me. I was trained for it really. Auntie Ginger – the second generation snob – so called because of her glorious long auburn hair (her real name was Ethel, after her doting mother, a name she disliked and rarely used) was the archetypal maiden aunt who wore Liberty skirts elasticated at the waist for comfort and who used bus journeys as a means to finish crocheting another ornament doily. Auntie would take me, her favourite niece, goddaughter and make-believe offspring on short bus-tour holidays whose success was judged not only by the quality of the finished needlework but also by the standard of the tea and its presentation at the various locations we visited on the trip.

This critical analysis characterised our inherited snobbery. Grandma had always insisted that everyone – everyone – drank tea from a cup and saucer, with the sole exception of Granddad when he came back from working down the pit who was then allowed a large mug of tea to quench his thirst. Even children had to have a cup and saucer. My mum would be in a mild state of rising panic.

"No," Grandma would be firm. "She won't drop it and she has to learn." She was right: I didn't drop it and I never forgot the trust I was given and the way it deepened my love for her.

How I Got my First Real Pet

Celeste Maguire was inspired by the sight of my black and white cat, which slept in the training room throughout our workshops. Notice how she has created a complete story here, with lots of authentic dialogue.

It's amazing what children will do when they really want something. I fell in love with Fluffy the minute I saw her, a tiny orange and white ball of fur tumbling through the neighboring farmer's cornfield. She was so sweet and cuddly. It was like holding a lovely warm stuffed animal that breathes. But how was I to keep her?

My father hated cats. "They're dirty and they claw the furniture."

As far as he was concerned, the closest we would get to having a pet was the occasional goldfish from the state fair, brought home in a plastic bag filled with water. But he hadn't counted on a little girl's love for a tiny fluffy kitten.

I brought Fluffy home and showed her to my mom, who immediately fell in love with her.

"Can I keep her, Mom?" I pleaded.

"You know how your father feels about having pets," she explained as she held the kitten in her arms, scratching under her white furry chin.

"But Mom, she's so tiny, she needs me. I'll take care of her all by myself. I promise! You won't even notice she's here."

"I'm sorry sweetheart, but you're going to have to take her back to the farm. She'll be happy there," she said sadly, handing Fluffy back to me with a sigh. But nothing could stop the quiet determination of a little girl who had fallen in love.

One rainy evening a few days later, my father pulled into the driveway around the back of the house. I heard the tires of his car crunching on the gravel and ran to the window, peeking behind the curtain, watching as he got out and ran towards the back door with a folded newspaper protecting his head from the rain.

Suddenly he stopped and looked around. As I carefully opened my bedroom window a crack, I heard a very distinct plaintive "meow".

"What in God's name is that?" he yelled, turning in the direction of our garbage cans. I watched my dad as he walked over to the cans and noticed one with the lid only partway on. "Damn kids! Why can't they put the lids on properly? The whole can is going to fill up with rain and garbage will be floating everywhere in the morning," he muttered as he started to put the lid on tight.

Once more a distinct "meow" could be heard, this one even louder than the first. I stood very still with only my head peeking out behind the curtain as my heart beat quickly, sucking on my fingers in fear as the drama below unfolded.

"What the hell!" he shouted as he lifted the garbage can lid and looked down. There was Fluffy, scared and a little bit wet, sitting on a soft blanket with a small saucer of milk.

As my father stared down at her in shock, it's as if she knew her life depended on this moment. Looking up at him with big blue eyes, she gave the most plaintive, sweet little meow man has ever heard. As he scooped her up into his arms, Fluffy nestled in as if she planned on lying there forever.

And that is how I got my first pet.

Fluffy lived for twenty years. Most of her evenings were spent sleeping on the sofa next to my dad as he watched television. I may have found her, but it was my dad who gave her a home.

Expecting

After one of my workshops Maggie Myklebust was inspired to write this. This is a super example of watching a cohesive piece of writing emerge from musing about something, in this case, pregnancy. Maggie weaves her own story with that of Adriana.

On Wednesday afternoon as I drove home from a writing session in Voorschoten, I felt deeply frustrated by my inability to spontaneously write. The assignment was easy enough: have a look around the room find something that inspires you and write. While everyone else sat around the table writing with frenzy, I came up empty. As I drove on, reassessing my situation I got an idea and it had been right there in front of me the whole time... Adriana.

She's one of the women at the writing workshop. Although she seems nice and is quite pretty, it's neither her looks nor her charm that inspire me, it's her condition.

Her belly swollen in its final stage of pregnancy gives an aura of magic, for very soon there will be a newborn child in her arms.

Wherever I go, whenever I see a woman expecting a child I stare in admiration. Contrary to belief that it was because of *Eve and that damn apple* that we women should suffer the punishment of birth, I believe it is a gift and has been rightfully bestowed on us. As women head down the same path towards motherhood, our journeys can be quite different, some much easier than others. Whether our method is natural, alternative or adoption the outcome is what's important.

I was lucky; my experiences in pregnancy were good. From the early inner secret to the growing anticipation of birth, I basked in contentment. Never feeling lonely and always reminded by the stirring within that I carried the future. With my maternal torch passed on to my daughters I have surprisingly found that a grandmother's love in every way rivals mothers'.

Having recently had my granddaughter here for a visit, I would read to her each night before bed. To my delight she picked Charlotte's Web, one of my favorites. Every night we'd eagerly crawl into bed. She would climb on to my lap and rest her head against my chest.

Holding the book in front so we both could see - her the pictures
me the words. I would read aloud and with the top of her head right
under my nose, the sweet smell of her hair reminds me of her mother, all
nestled in my lap reading Charlotte's Web a long time ago.

> *Life is always a rich and steady time when you are waiting for something
> to happen or to hatch.*   – E.B.White, *Charlotte's Web*

Carp in the Bathtub

**Fanny Bernstein, who is Dutch, of Polish descent, was inspired by the
cake she had been eating and that led her to think of the food of her
childhood. The dialogue is authentic. See how she calls her mother
Mama, just as she would have done back then.**

As in most Polish-Jewish families we ate gefillte fish nearly every Shabbath dinner. My mother
made real gefillte fish herself, of course from fresh carp, the head for my father and the minced
fish balls for us, the kids. But where could you buy fresh carp? At the market the carp was very
fresh, but they didn't have it every week. And so... because the fish had to be fresh, my dad
bought a living one! Yes, a real live carp!

I can still see it as clear as yesterday. Every Thursday evening my father came home with
a large bag, and there, inside, wrapped in lots of old newspapers, was a living – or, if you prefer
– a half dead carp, that was tossed straight into our bathtub. Meanwhile we could have a quiet
supper, and then afterwards his head would be chopped off by my mother's very own hands!

Every Thursday evening when my father came home he was greeted with the same
question: "Nuh and, any fresh carp today?" The answer to this question varied from week to
week. In the beginning my sister and I watched the carp swimming in our bathtub. It was
bizarre to see the bathtub we used so regularly, especially on Fridays before Shabbath, now
occupied by a shiny, slithering carp.

"That shiny skin is very important," Mama always said. "That shows you how fresh the
carp is."

After dinner and washing up the dishes my sister and I went to do our homework, or
sometimes we played for a while and then went off to bed. Mama went into the kitchen and
closed the door. But even through the closed door the rather 'special' smells of cooked fish
spread throughout our house.

I think I must have been around eight years old, and why, I really can't remember, but on
one Thursday evening, while the kitchen door was closed, I opened it and entered the kitchen.
And at that exact moment Mama gave the poor carp the deadly blow! The head flew off, the
tail moved heavily from right to left, and there was blood all over the kitchen sink and I... I
screamed! There was my mother, in the middle of the kitchen with her special big knife in her
hand that she only used for the fish. My mother, who was always sweet and soft, and with
whom I baked cookies and cakes, stood there with a huge knife in her hand. And she had used
it to kill the carp that I had just seen swimming happily in our bath! Completely shaken I ran
upstairs, to my room. Of course my father came and tried to console me.

"It is quite normal that human beings eat animals. Don't you eat every Friday evening a 'pulke' from the chicken, Fanny?" he said, sitting down beside me on the bed and patting my hand. He was right, the drumstick was my favourite piece of all and when my sister didn't want the other one, I would get both!

I don't remember how that evening ended. But I do know two things:
1)   I never ever entered the kitchen on a Thursday evening when the door was closed.
2)   I never ever ate gefillte fish again to this day.

Your task

Pick one of the memories you had when you completed the exercise, above, or another one that came to you while you followed the extracts, and write a story of 500-1000 words using the **seven steps for writing life story** and adding **SPICE**.

Seven steps to writing life stories

1. Compose
2. Review
3. Draft
4. Review
5. Polish
6. Revisit
7. Save

Spice up your life stories

- **S**pecifics
- **P**lace
- **I**ncident
- **C**haracter
- **E**motion

If you are taking the Personal Feedback Program

Please save and name your completed exercise using the YOURNAMETWO naming convention and email it to feedback@joparfitt.com

Your feedback will be returned to you within two weeks.

While you are waiting, feel free to move on to complete **Lesson Three - Writing about childhood**. It is recommended that you do not submit your homework for **Lesson Three** for **personal feedback** until you have received the feedback for this **Lesson Two**.

LESSON THREE

Writing about childhood

It should be easy, right? Writing about your childhood. You can remember the games you played and the key moments from the time when you were little. But, depending on how long ago your childhood was, it's pretty hard to recall the name of the girl who used to bully you so mercilessly or the actual clothes that the teacher you admired so much used to wear. You remember you had an argument with your mother, but you can't exactly remember the words she used. You know your bedroom was blue but you can no longer remember the colour of the carpet, what you had on the walls or the view from your window. That's the trouble with remembering events from so long ago: you can recall the general ideas but not the details, the faces and so on. The good news is that even without all these details, you can still evoke the time when you were growing up.

Think like a child

When you were a child, certain things interested you. The games you played, your friends, school, special food and maybe your grandparents. Perhaps you loved to dance or sing or make dens? Perhaps you loved to play with the bugs and beasties in the garden? Or perhaps you had long adventures in the fields on your bicycle or with your siblings? The things that matter to you now, like money and bills and house repairs, did not enter your head when you were little. You had different priorities. So, when you write about childhood, try to recall what mattered to you back then.

Speak like a child

Children use different language from adults. They can be more direct. They also use the slang and popular words of the time. So, ensure your children fit with the period.

Act like a child

Children often do not sit still; they can be constantly on the move. They fiddle with things, blurt things out or do things that are naughty. They can become absorbed in their own world for hours on end. Ensure the children you write about think, move and act like real children. The extracts in this lesson have been chosen because they will remind you what it is like to be a child.

Limbering up

1 Find a photograph of you when you were a child. Study the photograph carefully. Look at what you were wearing, the way you are standing, what you are doing, who is with you and examine the surroundings. How do you think you were feeling at this moment? How were the other people in the photograph, or in your life at the time feeling? Think about all this for a moment then take up your pen and write.

2 Write anything that comes into your head, inspired by this photograph. Write for as long as it takes. Don't worry about being perfect. Just write. Write it all down. Write yourself dry.

Extracts to inspire you

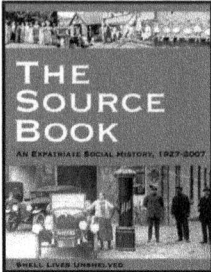

Extract – The Sourcebook, compiled by the Expatriate Archive Centre, EM, 0100/4/1/17.

Written by a child, this piece is a good reminder of the things that matter to you when you are young. It is very real.

Find out more about the archive at www.xpatarchive.com

I said goodbye to all the rooms in the house. It sounds crazy but I was only 9. I put my hand in the swimming pool and splashed the water saying goodbye. I explored the backyard and thought of thousands of memories. I rode my bicycle one more time around the backyard. The last thing I did in the house was get a pink post-it and write a note saying that whoever moves into my room must love it like I did and respect it. I stuck it on the wall and wanted to cry. I didn't cry.

Extract – Letters Never Sent by Ruth van Reken

Ruth van Reken wrote this when she was an adult, more than 30 years after it happened, yet she still evokes the way she felt when she was young, with the detail and emotion she felt keenly at the time.

Ruth's website is www.crossculturekid.org

September 1951

Dear Mom and Dad

There is one thing I think you'll be glad to know – I didn't suck my fingers when I went to sleep last night!

The kids say if the teachers catch you sucking your fingers, they'll tie a sock on your hand for a week. You have to keep it on all the time, even in class, and everyone laughs at you. I don't know how I could stop, because I haven't been able to all the times you've tried to make me. I finally decided to put my pillow by my feet, instead of under my head, so I couldn't rub my other hand under it like I always do. Then it wouldn't feel so cosy to suck my fingers either.

When Aunt Gert, our housemother, came by, she asked if I wanted the pillow, and I said I never use one. It was pretty hard to sleep without you or my pillow.

I want my mommy and daddy.

Love
Ruth Ellen

Dear Mom and Dad

I'm scared to death. I know I'm supposed to obey the rules, but there are lots more here than at home. I'm afraid I'm going to do something bad and get punished.

One of the worst rules is you can't get up to go to the bathroom during rest hour. I don't know why, but as soon as I lie down every day for my nap, I have to go. I've tried everything, but nothing helps. I drink only the tiniest bit of water or milk at lunch, but the minute I climb into bed for rest hour, I have to go. By the time the hour is over, it really hurts bad.

Yesterday I did a naughty thing. I thought I'd wet my bed for sure if I had to wait the last half hour, so instead, I used my wastebasket. I forgot I'd done it until I emptied the trash after school. Some spilled on me when I turned the wastebasket upside down!

I hope nobody finds out. I hate the idea that anybody besides you can punish me.

Love
Ruth Ellen

Extract – Black and Abroad by Carolyn Vines

Carolyn remembers her schooldays. She introduces us to her Spanish teacher, explaining how her love of Spanish was born. Notice the way she uses foreign words and also the way she invites the reader to pronounce the words.

Miss Wagner

There were no race riots at Northview, and I think our Vice-Principal was a Black man, so all of my worries were unfounded. I relaxed and started enjoying myself. I found my own way, without Dawn and Felicia, and while I didn't make any significant friendships with any of the White kids, I learned they weren't out to get me, either. My guidance counselor was supportive and my teachers seemed to take a liking to me, especially my Spanish teacher. To her face we all called her Senorita Wagner, but under my breath, I called her Saint Doris.

Every morning her Farrah Fawcett hair came bouncing into class followed by her mile-a-minute jibberish that in time would become my second language. Miss Wagner was in love with two things: Purdue University and all things Spanish, especially Josele Garza, a famous racecar driver. We were all in love with her.

She taught us how to play "*Olé*", which was her made-up version of "BINGO". She organized in-class talent shows. In one of them Tina and Pamela, the other two Black girls, and I sang a soul version of "Are You Sleeping Brother John" in Spanish. Not too many other kids growing up in the ghetto could say that. For an upcoming Parent Day, she asked us all to prepare a Spanish dish. I stole a dollar from my mother's purse to buy a package of shredded coconut, the main ingredient in *cocadas*, candies made by boiling water, adding sugar, and stirring in the coconut. When I bit into the first one I thought I had just swallowed a cup-full of sugar, and I was sucking the coconut out of my teeth for the rest of the day. To this day I can't stomach coconut, but I still love me some Spanish.

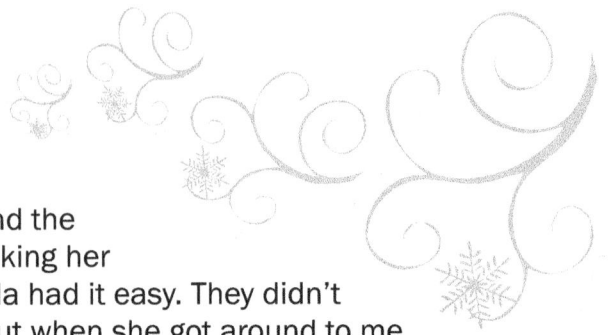

On the first day of class, Miss Wagner went around the classroom and one by one gave us our new names, flicking her feathered hair as she did it. My friends Tina and Pamela had it easy. They didn't really have to say their names differently in Spanish. But when she got around to me and said "Te llamas Carolina" my heart started pumping gallons of blood through my body, my eyes got big, and my fingernails found their way to my mouth. I was too embarrassed to say my new Spanish name.

I hated telling people my name in English. It was such a long and proper-sounding name. To most of the people, kids and some adults, the three syllables had been reduced to two: Curlyn. Every time I said Carolyn I just knew people were silently accusing me of "talking White".

So there I was, the center of attention, asked to pronounce four syllables and roll my "R". Miss Wagner insisted, firm but kind, that I say my name. "Caroleeena" was born that day. And whenever I was called on to answer a question, I spoke a language no-one else in The Retreat spoke; whenever I spoke Spanish, I knew I was prepared for the new world I was about to see.

My First Memory

Celeste Maguire uses the present tense, which makes it more immediate. Notice the details and the characterisation of her brother. The dialogue is authentic and has movement with it. Celeste paints us a clear picture of the scene and we can empathise with her easily.

I wake up as the sunlight is filtering through the blinds. As I turn my head, the pattern of small pink flowers on the wall feels so safe and familiar. Looking up, I see my bottle on the corner post of my crib. Yum! After pulling myself up with the help of the bars, I grab the bottle and take a big drink. Yuck! Ugh! It's sour!

With quiet determination fuelled by hunger and need, I climb over the side and slide down to the floor. Even as young as I am there is a feeling of pride of what a big girl I am, coupled with the fear of getting in trouble for climbing out. Toddling into the room next door in my PJ's with feet, carrying my bottle by the nipple, I see my mom and dad sitting up in a large bed reading a newspaper that is strewn over the spread. My mom looks at me, back at my dad, and sighs. I want a fresh bottle and I want my mommy and daddy. I can already picture myself snuggled between them, drinking the lovely warm liquid as they look down at me adoringly. Pure love. Pure bliss....

"You can't get in bed with us, you're wet!" cries my mom. "Bob, get your sister a bottle!" My big brother comes in resignedly, looks down at me and says, "I made her bottle last time."

"Just do it. Your father and I are trying to read the paper."

"All right, C'mon kid," says Bob, laying down the comic strips with a loud sigh and stomping out of the room.

I don't want to go with him. But as there is no choice I follow my brother into the kitchen and watch as he heats up a bottle in a pan of water on the stove. Feelings of rage and disappointment overwhelm me. I hate him already.

Grandma and my Green Friend

Adriana Volenikova, who is from Slovakia, wrote this piece about her childhood game. Notice how she includes the Slovakian words for her grandmother and the village, to add authenticity and to remind us of the setting. The atmosphere is very childlike and the tense is present, which draws us into the story.

He is green and fluffy with spiky edges. He has become my friend for a day and he is in desperate need of shelter. My grandma, whom I call Babka, is upstairs making her delicious sandwiches, out of white soft bread, filled with tons of butter, thin slices of turkey and salty cucumber, which she would later put into a wicker basket with a string tied to it. She would drop the basket and its contents down from her third floor balcony for me to enjoy without having to disrupt my shelter-building project.

"Adi, your sandwich is ready," comes a voice.

I look up. Babka's words spoken just loud enough to bring me back to reality and away from my animal kingdom. I have not even realized that I am hungry, though I am actually starving. After finishing my sandwich and sending back the wicker basket, I return to my green friend. My friend is a caterpillar and his home will be made out of wooden fence and green leaves. There is one giant leaf in the middle filled with some water, in case he gets thirsty. We play the whole day, in the shade of my grandma's house, as it is a bright and sunny day, with strong rays of sun that could burn his delicate skin. I needed to protect him, for he is my responsibility now.

With time and even days passing by, I decide that my guest needs friends and so I take him on a discovery journey looking for potential housemates. Snails, worms and other types of caterpillars seem like a perfect match. I bring them all some cabbage leaves for lunch from my grandma's fruit and vegetable shop in the village of Lednicke Rovne. Her shop seems more like a wooden hut than anything else. A hut that is too cold in winter yet too warm and humid in summer. But a hut, where my grandmother spent most of her adult life, selling fruit and vegetables, while secretly adding weight to all the produce as to charge just a little bit more to her customers. I am always fascinated by this tiny trickery.

"Grandma, why do you always add that tiny metal weight to every product?" I ask curiously.

"It seems like nothing, and it is nothing to every customer, but to me, over time, this adds up to a larger amount. I am simply doing what everyone else does in a different way," Grandma answers without hesitation or shame in her voice.

This is also a hut where I spend most of my school vacations, playing among wooden boxes, eating the entire heads of cabbages, until my stomach looks like one. It is lovely escaping the buzz of my hometown and spending so much time with my grandma in the simplicity of her village.

Your task

Write a story of 500-1000 words on your childhood using the **seven steps for writing life story** and adding **SPICE**. You could write about:

- Your first memory
- A defining moment
- Your grandparents or parents
- A letter to your parents when you were a child
- A game you used to play
- A childhood holiday
- Life at home

Seven steps to writing life stories

1. Compose
2. Review
3. Draft
4. Review
5. Polish
6. Revisit
7. Save

Spice up your life stories

- **S**pecifics
- **P**lace
- **I**ncident
- **C**haracter
- **E**motion

If you are taking the Personal Feedback Program

Please save and name your completed exercise using the YOURNAMETHREE naming convention and email it to feedback@joparfitt.com
Your feedback will be returned to you within two weeks.

Now move on to complete **Lesson Four - A sense of place**. It is recommended that you do not submit your homework for **Lesson Four** for **personal feedback** until you have received the feedback for this **Lesson Three**.

LESSON FOUR

A sense of place

You already know that you need to include a sense of place in your work, as Place is one of the elements of SPICE. In this lesson we are going to focus on setting the scene and creating a sense of place. Certain elements of SPICE are particularly useful here.

Specifics

Adding details where possible will help you set the scene. Name the flowers, name the city, the street, the drink, the restaurant, the people. Say 'Lagos' rather than simply 'African city'. If you use the words 'Boulevard Montparnasse' this evokes more than if you had written 'wide Parisian street'. Add Specifics to create a sense of Place.

Character

If you put a person into a scene, it can make that scene come alive, so remember to add Character, another element of SPICE.

Emotion

Evoke how you feel or the characters feel and you can add another dimension to the scene by adding Emotion, a further element of SPICE.

Readers are not mind readers

Ensure readers can **see** what you saw and **feel** what you felt and so on. Try to paint a picture with your pen. Using a metaphor or a simile to add details and description will help you to evoke the scene too. Take a look at the following examples:

The humidity was so high that it felt like a hot flannel had been thrown over my entire body.

The scent of frangipani was so thick with the perfume of sweet almond that you could slice it with a knife.

The dew-covered cobwebs looked like they had been spun with skeins of opals.

The hoar frost on a winter tree looked like the skinny black branches were dusted in icing sugar.

Lilac looks like wet mops in the rain.

Pollarded trees look like the limbs of lepers.

Limbering up

Let's practise this. Think of a time when you arrived somewhere new. It could be a new city, a new school or a new workplace, perhaps. Make a note here of what you noticed, using all your senses and finishing with a simile. For example, when I was newly arrived in Holland and felt a bit lonely I 'felt as if I were a windmill without any sails'. Try this now.

When I arrived. . .

1. I could see

2. I could hear

3. I could taste

4. I could feel

5. I could smell

6. It was as if

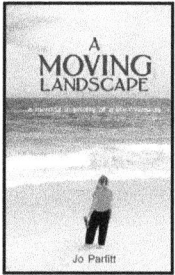

Extract – A Moving Landscape by Jo Parfitt

Setting the scene is not just about what you can see and describe. You can enhance the scene by adding details, people, dialogue, and a sense of culture, history or atmosphere. Notice how my poem below is filled with opinion, too, and how the language, the alliteration and assonance, can be used to further the setting of the scene.

Amstel Oasis

Dubai is in the desert –
but it isn't dry.
The sun scorches the unnatural flora –
that still receives a constant flow.
Palm trees, dressed in sackcloth,
beg the sky for rain
and it appears,
creeping humbly round their feet,
embarrassed by the modern means by which it came.

Bougainvillea flames purple,
clinging sheepishly to the walls of concrete playrooms,
coyly boasting verdance from inadvertent hoses.

Cranes and workmen build the ponds, the hills, the fast lanes,
planting grass greener than it ever shall be on the other side,
for it is fed and watered by some Sheikh's almighty hand.

Employment is international.
Only the blind beggar in his pram
needs hold out his hand.

Work while you are well.
The welfare state will never grow from lack of taxes.
While you are well there's a way to earn your bread –
be it pittance or golden-baked.

The world meets here.
Inside first class hotels,
lounging on the sundeck,
sipping Pimms through straws.
For here are exhibition halls,

conference rooms and swimming pools,
saunas, clubs and pubs.
Here is the home of the alcohol licence.
Here is the home of the Amstel can.

If you watch quietly,
you will see the Englishmen
neatly tuck their bellies into their trouser tops
and slowly fix their smiles and starry eyes
upon the taxi that takes them to their nightly wet dream.

Amstel Lite or Amstel plain?
We know when we will meet again
at Thatchers, Humphreys or the Falcon,
in the Odd Spot or Red Lion.
Tap your can to the music of the band,
live or pressed into a plastic disc,
or stretched inside a pirate tape
beside the video screen.

Home from home.
Without Saturday football by the telly,
feet on table, can on belly,
crisps crushed into the carpet
and lager to confuse the score.

Where is the real Dubai then?
Surely it cannot take the form of an Amstel swilling male
or a high thigh cut bikini strutting by the pool?
Then it must lurk behind those high walls and elegant gates,
flanked by oleander,
where the only peepshow comes from above.
Maybe this is where the dishdashed men and veiled women
carry out masked balls?

The people of the dhows cluster along Deiraside,
trading, transporting, carrying
on with life in a calm cross-legged way,
using their clothes as facecloths, then as towels,
shuffling towards their personal Nirvana,
wearing shapeless baggy suits,
commuting to the other side,
clinging like locusts to the abra's flesh.

Who will buy? Come and try. A look costs nothing
but we'll try to sell or haggle,

wash your car, be your barrow,
'Hello banana', 'Hello potato'.
Stallholders in the souk cry out for business,
polish up their apples, clean their peas and cues
and peel the skin from onions for humility.

Faded costumes, faded pride,
the locals step back to the shade,
conceal their thoughts and hide their heads,
leaving brightly coloured clothes for passing trade,
sitting on low stools
they lunch on samosa and Cherryade
and accept that it is they who are the foreigners.

Private people with a private alphabet,
anonymous dress and hidden homes,
saving bright lights and splendour for the mosques
and their energy for lilting prayer
to cool the mind and fill the air.

Perhaps they laugh at the blatant follies
of the bronzing beer men,
arrogantly driving to distance themselves
from these boozing bar men,
cleverly retaining anonymity
behind the same beard and the same wry smile,
sardonic in its reverence of the red-faced, peeling white man,
rushing to catch the last can of Amstel.

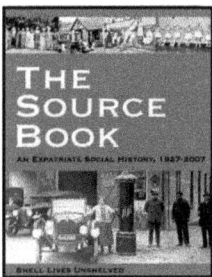

Extract – The Sourcebook, compiled by The Expatriate Archive
Centre, EvD-vL; Nigeria, 1992, 0901/359

This extract is filled with life and colour. Notice the senses of sound and smell are used as well as sight. There is a person in this piece and that person moves and talks, which gives an added dimension. The character of the taxi driver can be seen through his dialogue. See the short paragraphs and how this affects the pace.

Find out more about the archive at www.xpatarchive.com

Laughing at Tragedy

Lagos. On the way to the airport.

As always the traffic was heavy on the way to the airport and the progress slow. The atmosphere in the taxi was stuffy. We were packed together. My perspiration smells blended

with the typical Nigerian odour of the driver. He was wearing a colourful cap and moved his lips. I heard fragments of a song above the noise of the traffic around us.

Above our heads dangled gay-coloured decorations. The lively multi-coloured city life moved past my eyes. We drove past large office buildings, past slums built from waste material, past skilfully displayed fruits and past people sleeping on a piece of cardboard.

The road was bordered by strings of people; the colours of Nigerian men wearing pyjamas and women wrapped in cloths blended.

The sulky atmosphere made me sleepy.

Joltingly, the taxi came to a sudden stop. That was the last thing we needed: a traffic jam. The lorry in front of us was packed with Nigerians. If they had had more space, they would have doubled up with laughter. Something on the road was apparently very funny. It provoked my curiosity. What was so funny?

My readiness to join the laughers changed on the spot to feelings of horror, disgust, disbelief. On the tarmac a young Nigerian was stretched out. A car had knocked him down and crushed his head. No blood, only this flat head, distorted, grotesque.

Cars slowly passed the body, people pointed at it, laughing. I shuddered at the sight. Did not understand it.

"Why do they laugh?" I asked the driver.

He shrugged his shoulders, "Should they cry? Does it matter?" he said.

This gave me something to think about during the long ride to the airport. And I have been thinking about it ever since.

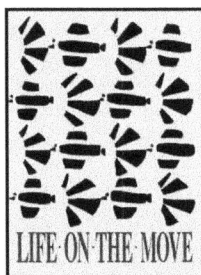

Extract – Life on the Move, compiled by The Expatriate Archive Centre, Nigeria 1973, translated

Again we go to Lagos and see and smell and hear all that is going on in this rich piece set in the early 1970s. The author's feelings are clear and the details lend much to the scene.

Find out more about the archive at www.xpatarchive.com

Lagos Market

I loved the mixture of goods, the smell of food, the laughing and quarrelling of the women. The markets were mostly run by women. The ones in charge looked impressive, queens they were, wearing richly embroidered cloths, draped in many layers around the waist. They wore the multi-coloured, stiff head-dress as if it were a crown.

Once a Nigerian mother drew my attention laughingly and made clear by sign language that I could have her baby in exchange for my handbag. I took over the chubby little cherub and gave her my handbag; we both knew it was a joke. It was a pleasure, the feeling of this small, warm and dark body, dressed in not more than a string of beads, in my arms. I strolled past the stalls, was met with laughter and white flickering teeth. I regretted giving back the baby to his mother in return for my handbag. No need to check the contents. I knew there was nothing missing.

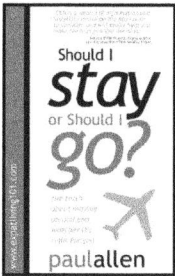

Extract – Should I Stay or Should I Go? by
Paul Allen

Here the comparison is made between the heat of San Diego, New York and England. Notice how Paul describes the weather clearly and concisely and how by describing how the heat affects the people who live there and how it feels we can truly understand.

Paul's website is www.expatliving101.com

When I visited my friends in San Diego it was August. For all that month we had blue skies every single day. Not a drop of rain. Barely even a cloud. And the temperatures were up around 100°F throughout.

Yet when I got there I was surprised to find my friends, and everyone we met, spent virtually all day inside. They were holed up like moles with the windows and doors shut, blinds down and the air conditioning pumping out.

Coming from gloomy England to this paradise of sunshine I couldn't believe it at first. Wasn't that California's lure? The clear skies, the warmth, the opportunity to live life in the great outdoors?

It didn't take long to understand why though. It was simply too hot, and the sun too fierce, to spend the day – especially early afternoon – outside.

Summers in New York were similar, with a hundred degree humidity added in for good measure. Stepping outside was like having a bucket of warm water thrown over you. Any form of exertion – even if it was a walk to the end of the next block – left me dripping with sweat.

Meet and Heat

Sandra Forbes and her family lived in China for a while. See how the use of local sayings has been used to add atmosphere and humour. Again, we have a character in the piece, which makes it easier to add that all-important dialogue.

The dog dangled from the hook, the last drips of blood from the hole in its head coagulating across its already furless body. Below, the yelp of puppies, should the shopper prefer to kill their own, panted in the early morning heat.

This was my second day in Guangzhou, Canton, where they eat 'all that flies except the aeroplane' and 'everything with legs except the table'.

"Come to market, Sandra," my new Aussie friend, Kathy, had said. "We need to get it over with. The first time is always the worst."

Kathy had been correct in every way. Was I horrified! Thank God for jet lag. My body felt like it hadn't hit earth yet and so, fortunately, I felt like I was dreaming throughout the experience. It was hotter inside the market than out. And outside was about 36 degrees.

We pushed our sunglasses up and back to hold our dripping hair and headed for the fish section, passing both live and dead cats, rats and a stall of hats. It looked like the fish were swimming in lukewarm water. They had to be, in that heat.

"Aagh," I exclaimed as a large empty-bellied catfish, still moving, slid off the board away from the chopper that had just gutted it, hit my leg and gave its last flap at my feet.

Rodeo

Laura Stephens is British, lives in Houston and wrote the following extract from her forthcoming memoir. See how she paints a vivid picture of the scene, the people and what is going on around her. She uses her own family so that we can see the scene through their eyes and uses strangers to show another side to the culture. The dialogue is authentic and adds both reality and humour. By describing a few incidents like this, we get a glimpse of the rodeo for ourselves.

Laura's blog is at http://laurajstephens.wordpress.com

We arrive at the Reliant Stadium and join the dense crowd snaking around the auditorium. The sounds are chirpy and chaotic, stalls selling colourful t-shirts and racks of baseball caps line the route. Excited little cowboys and cowgirls wear Stetsons edged with tinsel. The smell of hot dogs and sweet popcorn mingle around us making me suddenly ravenous. I'm aware of my metal watchstrap that has slid down my wrist from perspiration.

Locating our aisle, we pause at the top of the steep steps leading down to the stadium. Inside it is vast and yet surprisingly cool, courtesy no doubt of the sealed roof and air conditioning. White, red and blue, flags flutter gracefully above us – half are the American flag, the others bear the white star of Texas against red, white and blue rectangles – each one is big enough to cover a tennis court.

"Look, Mum," Megan's brown arm points upwards. Her mouth is open slightly, "show-offy flags!"

Vendors wear white flared pants, trimmed with cerise rhinestones and carry boxes of food slung around the waist. After nearly two years in Texas, I finally understand what they are saying.

"Come on y'all and git yur eats." They hold up their wares; bags of cotton candy, peanuts, Dr Pepper sodas and chilled Budweiser.

We find our four plastic, moulded seats among the crowd of mums and children. The girls have counted off the weeks, then the days from the international school calendar pinned to the corkboard on our American fridge. Now finally they will get to see their teen idol, Miley Cyrus.

Megan, our middle child, sits between her sisters holding a polystyrene tray; they help themselves to refried beans with melted cheese, spread over a layer of corn chips. They each have a bucket size soda with a foot long straw poking out – enough to hydrate a whole playground of kids for only a couple of dollars each.

Far below us, a rodeo starts.

"What's going on?" Megan asks.

"Um not sure," I hesitate, "it looks like we're going to see some rodeo after all. There had

been no mention of three hours of livestock action before Miss Cyrus came on stage – I wish I'd known, I could have warned the girls what to expect.

"I thought rodeos were in fields," Megan says.

She has a point. Knowing the concert was inside the Reliant Stadium I hadn't anticipated the livestock coming indoors!

"We're lucky to catch the rodeo," I offer optimistically.

Megan pauses for a moment of reflection.

"OK, but when's Miley coming on?"

We are interrupted by a burst of activity on the floor of the stadium. A lone calf zigzags crazily around an enormous pen. A cowboy shoots out from a hidden entrance at the side. His Stetson flays back and forth wildly as his long, blue-jeaned legs grip the girth of his chestnut horse; hooves rhythmically pound out a large circle around the calf. His right arm rotates aloft, whipping the air with his lasso.

In one swift, balletic movement the calf snaps, upended onto his spine. His hooves pointed skyward, his body inert forming a triangle shape.

I glance at Elen. The corn chip nestled in her little cherub hand stops halfway to her mouth. Her blue glass marble eyes, hold their gaze on the hapless calf. The colour is still draining from her face as she says in a small voice, "is he dead?"

"No, no sweetheart, he's just caught in the cowboy's rope. He's showing how clever he is at lassoing," I say.

"But he's dead, he's not moving, Mummy," says Elen.

"It's okay, it's the cowboy's job to look after his animals and make sure they don't run off."

My hand reaches over the arm of the seat, I place it on her leg. "He'll be fine in a minute."

Elen's soft hand closes over mine. The corn chip falls to the floor forgotten.

Arrival in Zambia

Trish Huisman wrote about arriving in Zambia in 1975. We can see the scene clearly and this is made even more vivid by the introduction of and interaction with Sister Azalina. By using Sister Azalina to introduce us to the house you see a novel way of describing a scene through the eyes of a character.

The parched ground beneath us is a warning of the stifling air, which will greet us when the doors of our small Zambia Airways plane are opened.

Phew! We are back in Africa. The heat, the smells, the chattering all around us and the pink bougainvillea trailing over the front of the small Arrivals Hall.

"There she is!" calls my husband. "That's Sister Azalina." She's approaching quickly, her coal black face gleaming beneath her super-white habit and giving us a huge, bright smile.

"Welcome to Ndola," she says as she clasps our hands in the traditional handshake.

"There's the Mission Landrover, over there." She points to a mud covered, battered vehicle standing nearby.

We begin our 200 kilometre drive along the tar strip road and count ourselves lucky that we don't have to carry all our luggage in the same way as the locals.

"Just look at those women," I comment. "How on earth do they balance those baskets on their heads?"

"Oh," answers Sister Azalina casually, "they've been doing that since childhood."

"And do they always dress so colourfully?" I ask her, feeling drab in my plain white tee shirt and black trousers.

"Yes, Mrs. Doctor. The *chitenga* is their normal dress and it's a sort of wrap-around cloth," she replies. "Very easy to wear."

About two hours later, we turn right, down a very bumpy lane, passing several straw-hut villages on the way and come to a stop outside a long, low bungalow.

"This is your home. Welcome to Mpanshya," says Sister Azalina smiling broadly. We enter a small red-tiled kitchen with a wood-burning stove in the corner. There's a large stone sink with a mosquito net protected window above it. Then, through into a little dining/sitting room with its highly polished stone floor. Nice and cool, I think to myself. Before we're introduced to our bedroom Sister Azalina explains how we will have electricity for a couple of hours a day as the generator cannot provide more and water can be heated by feeding the stove with wood that will be provided by Wonga and/with his wheelbarrow on a daily basis.

"Always check for snakes on your doorstep before stepping out and we are visited by game now and then," she continues. "There are a few lions, leopards and so on. Not many. We've just cooked some elephant meat stew for the hospital as one was shot the other day after marauding and causing serious damage in the villages here."

She pauses and turns to my husband. "Let's go and introduce you to the hospital now and you can meet some of the nurses and patients. There are about 80 at the moment so we're quite busy." My husband is the only doctor and as I stare through the mosquito netted window, taking in the frangipani bush opposite, I can't help thinking that the coming three years are perhaps going to be quite challenging. A tingling feeling of excitement goes right through my body.

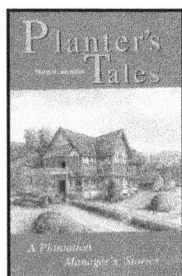

Extract – Planter's Tales by Mahbob Abdullah

The author's description here is carefully written and the names of people and places add authenticity. See, again, like in the piece, above, how a character is used to expand on the description.

A Short Friendship

It was some weeks before I got round to visiting Alex on his island. One day I got the operator to send a radio message to say I was arriving on the copra boat "Kelly" the next morning. It went the long way around the shallow reef. As it was not as fast as a canoe, it gave me time to take in the leaning palms over Lever Point, with white crests of waves washing the shore. In the shallows, the water changed colour to light green. Further into the sea where the water was

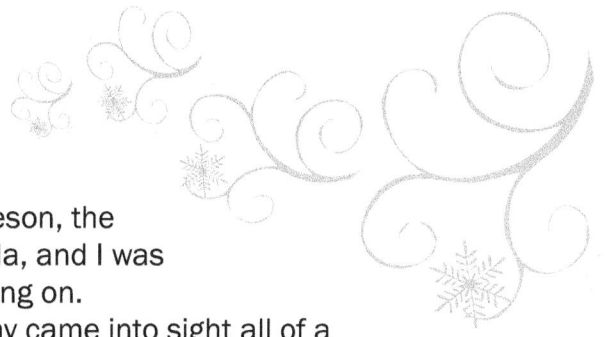

deep blue, I pointed to a horde of diving seagulls. Patteson, the boat captain, smiled, as he kept his course for Pepesala, and I was left to wonder what type of fish the seagulls were feeding on.

Pepesala was on Pavuvu Island, and Pepesala bay came into sight all of a sudden. When the boat turned beyond Pavuvu point, the bay opened like a crescent of pale green water. Coconut palms grew in lines, tall and slanting all along the shore with more straight lines on the slopes. The only gap was where a long wooden bungalow stood in the middle of the curve, with a front lawn that led to the jetty. From the bay the bungalow was a small white building. Nevertheless the scene got better and better as I got near. Under a blue sky, and a green sea and with a manta ray winging away from below the boat, I absorbed the best scenery in the world that I knew.

Alex waited at the jetty, and as we walked up the front lawn amidst the smell of new mown grass, I observed him, a kind of slightly bended knee type of walk, as if he was stalking something important. But it was only his excitement because he had already laid out a program that would begin after we had coffee.

Your task

Where do you live now? What kind of house is it? What kind of neighbourhood? What kind of people live there? What do they eat? What happens there? What does it look like? How does living there affect you or the people who live there? How would someone else describe it? Write a story of 500-1000 words that takes me into your current world. Use the **seven steps for writing life story** and add **SPICE**.

Seven steps to writing life stories

1. Compose
2. Review
3. Draft
4. Review
5. Polish
6. Revisit
7. Save

Spice up your life stories

- **S**pecifics
- **P**lace
- **I**ncident
- **C**haracter
- **E**motion

If you are taking the Personal Feedback Program

Please save and name your completed exercise using the YOURNAMEFOUR naming convention and email it to feedback@joparfitt.com

Now move on to complete **Lesson Five - Writing about people.** Wait to submit your homework for **Lesson Five** until you have received your graded homework from this lesson.

LESSON FIVE

Writing about people

Character is another element of SPICE. In this lesson we will focus on how to write compelling characters in your stories.

People move, talk and have feelings. How people interact with you helps to show the reader more about you. How your characters interact with each other reveals more of their personalities.

When you set the scene for your story, you paint a picture with your pen and show the reader what you saw, share the tastes, sounds and smells too. But when you add a person to your story, it can bring the piece to life. A story about London can include the architecture, the Thames, black cabs and red buses, busy streets and strap-hanging on the tube. Include a little girl feeding the pigeons in Trafalgar Square or an old lady sitting on a bench beside the Serpentine, eating a small pot of strawberry yoghurt and your writing gains another dimension.

People make your stories stronger, more vibrant and more interesting. Let's explore how you can do that.

In *Tales from the Expat Harem* Wendy Fox describes her first experience of a Turkish bath, or *hammam*. She could have simply told us that the place was filled with old ladies and children, instead she writes:

'Inside the main chamber, there were females of all ages, ranging from chubby toddlers, with perfect skin slippery as melting chocolate, to the very elderly, with bony backs bent into a comma, hair rusty with henna.'

Now we can see the children, and the *hammam* comes to life. We can picture the smooth-skinned toddlers and the way the old ladies move over the damp floor.

Every time you set a scene, the chances are that you were not the only person present. Show the other people too.

Adding traits to characters

Here is a list of some of the things you could use to describe your character and make him or her come to life:

- First name
- Surname
- Label, such as teenager, midwife, taxi driver, waiter, Goth

- Identifying mark, such as a bald head, a big nose, a gap in his teeth or straight shoulders

- Descriptive adjective, such as tall, short, skinny, uncomfortable, obese, talkative, uneducated, blonde

- Quirk, such as a twitch, a limp, a brusque manner, a stutter, over-enthusiasm

- Habit, such as drinking large mugs of tea, interrupting, repeating themselves, cycling everywhere

- Way of speaking, maybe he says 'eh?' or 'innit' at the end of a sentence, uses clichés or very long words

- Way of moving. Perhaps they had a limp, or strode about, or had flailing limbs

- Action, maybe he is drinking tea, digging a flowerbed, driving a car, so that while he talks he can lift a cup, slurp, shove a spade into soil, move the gear lever

- Clothing, could be a tweed jacket, blue overalls, a black beret, miniskirt or thigh-length boots

- Context, either add a person to a scene, or add a scene to a person

- Relationship with you, maybe it is polite, rude, a victim and persecutor partnership, best friends, confidantes, teacher and pupil, chilly, distant, warm and friendly

All the examples above could be used to help your character come to life. Do not try to use every example for every character you include, but try to help the reader visualise each person in some way.

See how the following examples illustrate how much more effective a piece of writing is when there is a character and that character comes to life:

The beach was almost deserted at sunset. And as the amber disc became a semicircle and then slipped away behind the ocean's shelf, I revelled in the peace and beauty of the scene.

Then we add people:

The beach was almost deserted at sunset. And as the amber disc became a semicircle and then slipped away behind the ocean's shelf I revelled in the peace and beauty of the scene. Except for one other family, I was alone.

Then we give the people an identity so the reader can see them:

The beach was almost deserted at sunset. And as the amber disc became a semicircle and then slipped away behind the ocean's shelf, I revelled in the peace and beauty of the scene. Except for a young family of four, who stood in a line holding hands and paddling in the shallows, I was alone.

See what happens when we add some dialogue and a bit more action:

The beach was almost deserted at sunset. And as the amber disc became a semicircle and then slipped away behind the ocean's shelf, I revelled in the peace and beauty of the scene. Except for a young family of four, who stood in a line, holding hands and paddling in the shallows, I was alone.

*   "Papa! Viens!" called the smallest boy. Broken away from the group, he was racing through gentle waves towards a rock. There were bound to be crabs lurking beneath it. There always were.*

*   French, eh? I've always found it so gratifying to see that foreigners come to spend their summers in the place I've lived all my life. I love it here. I've never wanted to leave Cornwall.*

Adding the dialogue and action gives the writer the chance to reflect on what she sees and share more of her own story. The family can be used to share more description, in this case rocks and crabs. And now we know that the scene is in Cornwall and that the writer loves living there. Now the scene is set you could continue with your story.

How to write dialogue

One of the hardest things to learn when you are writing stories is the punctuation and layout. Here, below, are some tips and rules to help you get it right.

When you have a piece of dialogue, it is advisable to start a new line with it. Start a new paragraph or start a new line and indent the text for the dialogue. It breaks up the solid prose of your piece and shows the reader that something fun is about to start. Readers like to see dialogue on a page because it looks more fun than solid prose. Do not feel obliged to start a new line for each piece of dialogue. You can start it mid-line, but I prefer not to do that. Let me show you what I mean:

Using indent

Jane stood on the shore beside the lake and dipped her bare feet into the shallow water. Her red toenails sank immediately into the sand.
*   "Ugh! It's muddy," she said with a shudder. But she stayed there wiggling her toes.*

Using a new paragraph

Jane stood on the shore beside the lake and dipped her bare feet into the shallow water. Her red toenails sank immediately into the sand.

"Ugh! It's muddy," she said with a shudder. But she stayed there wiggling her toes.

Starting mid-line

Jane stood on the shore beside the lake and dipped her bare feet into the shallow water. Her red toenails sank immediately into the sand. She shuddered and said, "ugh! It's muddy." But she stayed there wiggling her toes.

Notice the placement of the inverted commas, or quotation marks, and the commas, exclamation marks and full stops in the above examples.

Punctuating dialogue

There are rules for punctuating dialogue. Here are some examples to help you:

Punctuation comes inside the closing inverted comma:

"I hate fish," Jenny said.

When the sentence does not end with the dialogue, use a lower case first letter for the first word that comes after the closing inverted commas. If the word following the dialogue is a proper name, use a capital.

If the sentence ends with the dialogue, then you start the next sentence with a capital in the normal way:

"I hate fish," she said.

"I hate fish," Jenny said.

"I hate fish!" she said.

"I hate fish!" Jenny said.

"Do you hate fish?" he asked.

"Do you hate fish?" John asked.

"I will not eat this fish." Jenny put down her knife and fork, folded her arms and leaned back in her chair.

"I will not eat this fish." She put down her knife and fork, folded her arms and leaned back in her chair.

Senses and similes

When you are describing something, a person, remember to think about including elements of the five senses:

- Sight
- Sound
- Smell
- Taste
- Touch

I am not suggesting that you add all five to every description of every person, but do try to use a variety of methods to paint a picture of the people you include. Use them carefully to evoke as much as you can in few words.

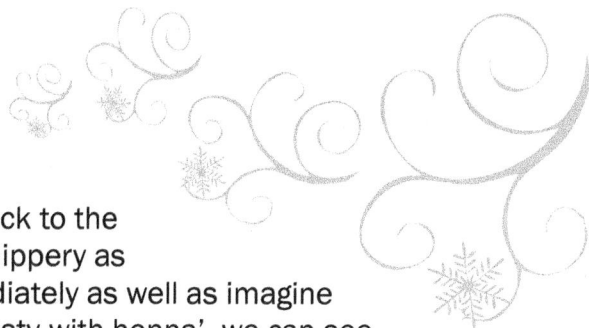

Use similes and metaphors, though sparingly. Think back to the hammam story above. Fox describes the children as 'slippery as melting chocolate', which allows us to see them immediately as well as imagine what they feel like to the touch. Similarly, in her 'hair rusty with henna', we can see it, imagine what it feels like and surmise the age of the 'elderly' ladies.

Symbols

Try using some dramatic licence to add symbols to your work to evoke the mood in a subtle way. The French author Gustave Flaubert was excellent at this. He would have Emma Bovary wearing a yellow dress on a sunny day when she was happy and watching butterflies flying upwards to increase the impression of her happiness.

Use the surroundings, weather, clothing and so on as symbols and metaphors when possible. Consider the following examples of the use of symbols to describe school children who are having a tough time in a new foreign school:

- *Nikita knocked on my door on one of the hottest days of the year, but the look on her sad face made me freeze for a moment.*

- *Anyone who saw Jack in the school corridor always noticed his huge baggy jeans, which hung in folds on his skinny frame, before they looked at his face.*

- *Tom was a popular boy. The kind who was captain of every team and always took the lead in the school play.*

Try to help your reader to be there with you and understand every situation perfectly. Make sure that your description and style are appropriate to your reader.

Interviewing people

You may want to interview people in order to include their stories in your writing too. Perhaps you want to talk to your aged aunt to find out more about your late father's childhood? Or maybe you want to interview someone and write a case study of him or her for a book, article or blog?

An interview will only ever be as good as the questions you ask. Devise your questions carefully and ensure that they will elicit the responses you need. In a nutshell, appropriate interviews take into account that you:

- Ask the right questions.

- Know what content you are looking to achieve.

- Ask your interviewees to tell you more when they share something interesting, including:

  - How that made them feel
  - How it may have changed them
  - What the people they talk about looked like, their quirks, clothes, how they spoke, what they did

- What the scenes in which action took place looked like. Ask your interviewees to paint a picture: what was on the wall, what was the carpet like, the décor, the view, the smell and so on

- Ask open questions, ones that produce full sentence answers not 'yes' or 'no'.

- And while you are talking, you need to take notes of the details and interesting information that will give your writing colour, but you also need to go 'Quote Spotting'.

Quote spotting

Once you have prepared thoroughly for your interview, you need to get the best out of your conversation. I always tell my students that it is not necessary to write down every word they hear but, instead, to go what I call 'Quote Spotting'.

Listen out for the important things people say and the full, interesting sentences that you know will embellish your text, endorse your point and look good on the page.

Begin each interview by making a note of the date and place of the conversation and check you have spelled the name of the interviewee accurately. Before continuing, ensure they know that the material may end up in print, so check if they are happy to be named or prefer that you use a pseudonym.

It is worth making a few notes about your interviewee's personality and the surroundings in which you find yourself as some of this could be useful when you later put the comments into context.

If you plan to publish your memoir someday, then keep your notes in a safe place just in case, on publication, any issues arise as to the truth of your published comments. You may need to prove that what was said, really was said.

Limbering up

Let's practise this.

Look back into your past and think of a significant person from your childhood. Perhaps your mother, father, grandparent, carer or sibling? Now complete the following chart, noting the following details about them.

Their name

Their relationship to you

Describe the clothes they would typically wear

Do they have any traits, ways of moving, quirks or mannerisms?

Briefly describe a place where they feel at home. The kitchen, garden, church or office maybe.

What do they typically do in that place? What movements do they make?

What typical phrases do they use?

How do you interact with that person? What do you say to each other?

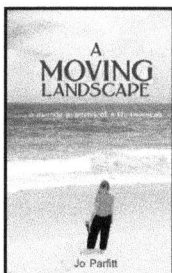

Extract – A Moving Landscape by Jo Parfitt

In this poem about my mother, notice how I describe her by putting her into the scenes I consider to be typical.

Busy

I'll find you in the garden,
your hands streaked black with soil,
poking fragile roots into trowelled holes.
Push your fingers into autumn briars,
stain them red and black with berries,
loving all that grows
on ground and tree or in the hedgerow.

I'll find you in the country lane,
dog lead swinging from your pocket,
and you, deep in conversation with a neighbour, friend or postman
laugh oblivious to the escaped dog
and the car slamming on its brakes.
Clap your hands and whistle!
The English Cocker trots closer,
feathers and ears flying
and you whelp with pride
as wet paws prick, sliding
muddily on your thighs.
'Good girl!' you say,
patting hard her silken back.
Her wagging tail seems fit to snap.

I'll find you by the pulpit,
buckets crammed with red and green,
bursts of yellowgold and cream.
Standing back, considering
the lilies on the font
in all their glory.

I'll find you at your easel,
low stool balancing on sand
as you paint the sea in pastels
drawing passion with your hand.

I'll find you on the swingseat,
lulled gently by a glass of wine,
eyes closed and face upturned
to the evening sun
that dips below the rooftops as
you sip the drink you've earned.

I'll find you on the sofa,
damp dog spooning at your side
and a welcome sherry
a pleasure impossible to deny.
A second glass sits empty on the leather top
of a small round table as your husband of fifty years,
my father, head flopped back like a hinge,
sleeps and snores. Silent, breathless
before each almighty explosion
that you just ignore.
You'd rather watch the flames of a living fire.
Jessie, pressed against you,
prods you with her paw.
You set down your drink
and stroke her willingly.

I'll find you in the mirror
when I trace the lines upon my face.
And I find you when my children
stoop to kiss you and embrace.
You're in my words, my lips, my head,
my love of cheese with fresh French bread.
At my shoulder by the stove,
reminding me that I should use
'five, three and two' for crumble,
'four, four and two' for cake.
You're in every dish I make
and blackened on the base of each burnt pan –
a memory that will not scrape away.

I find you there in every sigh
that's glad we'll have a sunny day.
'Oh boy, this'll do chaps.'
'This is just the job,'
as stripping off the layers of cloth
you turn your face up to the sun
and thank the Lord for what he's done.

Extract – Planter's Tales
by Mahbob Abdullah

Mr Veloo works on a tea plantation in Malaysia. Here we get to meet him and see his relationship with his work, his colleagues and his wife.

Mr Veloo

Mr. Veloo was the conductor on Cashwood Estate, about 2,000 acres of rubber in the state of Oerak in Malaysia. With the estate managed by Harrisons and Crosfield, the standards were high. I was proud to be accepted as a management trainee. As Mr. Veloo was in charge of tapping I could learn a lot from him. I had followed his stout figure into the fields and watched him find the tappers, checking on the tasks for bark consumption with a tape he carried with him, sticking a knife tip to see the depth of tapping. He would check the angle of the panel slope and use his tapping knife to correct the back-channel. Some trees were untapped, and he would test the panel with a cut to see if the tapper was deliberately missing a good tree.

In all the days that I was with him, Veloo was patient, smiling and had a good word for every tapper. Even when he scolded, it was in a persuasive way. Veloo had never been angry, despite the hard pace he set for himself. He did not get excited but stayed calm and he did not sweat. He was only slightly cross when I lingered too long at the task of Kuppoo, the most beautiful tapper in the estate, her lean figure clearly outlined by her clean sari, her naked midriff slim. Her thick raven hair fell across the panel as she tapped. Mr. Veloo told me to hurry up; there was more work to do.

As I rode pillion on his old Honda Cub, his tapping knife rattling in the wire basket, he would speed, with him leaning slightly forward as if willing the machine to go just that little bit faster.

Learning from Veloo was a long process. The office work involved a lot of figures, and it took a long time to go through them. It was good to leave the work and go to his house for tea, where his two sons, Jegatheson and Ramesh would crawl all over him. His wife pampered him with more cakes. At night, under the fluorescent lights and flying insects, he and Mr. Varkey the manager of the co-operative shop would play badminton at the court in front of the house. Here Veloo would sweat a little. I played sometimes when the spirit moved me, but soon I would go back to the comfort of the Assistant's bungalow in which I was allowed to stay.

The Twisted Moustache
by Sandra Forbes

This description of her stepfather comes to her in a flashback.
Her feelings are made clear in this poignant piece.

As the rain became icy cold trickling down the gap between my hat and the collar of my raincoat, I diverted my attention and began to window shop.

I passed my third designer store and was distracted by a red and white twisted pole above a small window. Inside I could see a barber styling the beard of a large portly man. I froze. For an instant my brain played tricks with me. It couldn't be? He has been dead for is it 19 or 20 years?

I shivered. Was it because of the rain or the emotions that swept through my body, as my memory played tricks on me? For an instant I thought it was him.

My stepfather had a flowing grey to white beard with a moustache that he twisted at the ends. He was a large man with a twinkle in his deep brown eyes and a huge character unique to him. Anyone who knew him could tell when he was near, even if they could not see him, due to the smell of St Bruno wafting from his pipe. In the evening a large King Edward cigar could often be found dangling from his mouth. The smoke would curl above his head in the shape of a small circle growing larger and larger until finally it was forced to break up and eventually disappear completely.

This large Father Christmas like character had a heart as big as a bucket. In our town everyone knew him as a lovable rogue, easy to get on with but not to be crossed.

As I stood there, the rain now long forgotten, I felt many stages of sadness and joy. I remembered the things he and I got up to. From the day I sat on his lap feeling safe and secure, twiddling his beard with my tiny fingers to the final farewell.

The wider than normal coffin draped with the military flag of his regiment. The bearers standing so proud as they lifted him high. They would rather have been court martialled than to let their knees start to buckle. I imagined him lying there with his pipe and baccy and wondered if he could see us all saying goodbye. He would have had a great laugh at the people below (or would he have been looking up) all there because of him. He would have been very proud to realise just how much he was loved.

Suddenly the sound of the large doors thudded shut behind me. I realised this was it, my time to give a silent goodbye. As the deep blue curtains closed around him I gave a little grin. I hope they remembered to twist his moustache.

My Happy Green Day

Ellen Rosina, who is from Aruba wrote this about her mother. Her language here is very natural and the character of Ellen's mother is made very clear through their interaction.

At the age of 17, I was a rebellious, stubborn and determined teenager.

My mother always complained at my odd way of doing things and I had a problem with her dominant attitude.

Sometimes I had the feeling that she favoured my sister above me or that she really didn't know who I was, or did not care or didn't have time to consider my feelings and that really worried me.

My mom had these strict rules, she always was on my case:
"Rosaline . . . come inside! Rosaline . . . it's 9 o'clock, put off the light and go to sleep. Rosaline . . . sweep the house before you go to school. Rosaline . . . put on the stove. Rosaline . . . I said No!"

In the morning time, I used to see all my neighbours' children and my school friends passing by going to school, while I had to do some chores before I left to school and that used to create an inner hate. Tchuh . . . that woman, my mother . . . she is really disgusting. I used to grind my teeth and make a fist but didn't dare to backchat her and surely not in the morning time because I knew what was coming to me, if I dared answer back.

Sometimes I used to hate her for being my mother, she was so strict. Mostly all of my friends could just tell their parents if they were planning to go to a party or any other activities, but I . . . oh no! I had to beg and behave myself days ahead very nicely and try to not make any mistakes otherwise the deal of going out could just be over in a few seconds, just like that.

Whenever I wanted to go somewhere, I had to be very careful with my words. During those days I had to walk on the tip of my toes and swallow all kinds of crap sent in my direction. Sometimes I really felt like exploding, but I always used to think, one day this shit will be over. One day I will be free of this golden-chained gate.

Why I Cannot Say "I love you"

This powerful piece paints a vivid picture of Cecilia's relationship with her mother and how her mother's actions affected her as a young child. Notice the use of present tense and the strong feelings she expresses. The dialogue has been taken from typical phrases her mother used to say.

Cecilia's website is www.ahimsa-satya.com

I don't even know the colour of your eyes. I know that dark look; the wrinkle between your eyebrows creasing so hard it turns into one large crevasse. I know the anger coming out of

your eyes, while your back is hunching. I know the blow that will come next. Never to my face – I always manage to get my head out of the way first.

I don't know what is worse – the physical blows or the verbal ones. The latter spewing from your mouth like the snakes out of Medusa's head, their vile tongues spreading venom in the form of words. They actually hurt more than the physical blows as they hit straight in the heart – like a bee sting right between the breasts. There is no protection from these, no hands to protect or to strike back.

My body is getting stronger and I will be able to hit back one day, but my heart and mind are too young to understand why or how words can hurt this much.

"You will never ever find somebody," is how the rant usually starts.

I am heading for the front door, opening the drawer to get my hat and gloves out of the low brown bureau in our hallway.

"You will always be alone," your mouth spews out, your hands grabbing for my coat on the hanger to make sure that I can't put it on and leave before you are finished with spreading your poison.

"Nobody will ever want to be with anyone like you," the last stab before I have my coat and can run down the stairs, tears and anger in a wild mix moving me forward, away, fast.

As I make a lot of friends at school, in the choir, at badminton, on our street you need to change your tactics. So when I am around 14 this turns into: "you are sick in the head. You need to see a doctor," followed by the Medusa head taking a step back, watching me from a distance, slightly tilting back before the last thrust of: "you are not OK."

That summer you make me buy my own toilet paper and menstruation pads from the money I make with my first summer job, directing one of the many-more-to-come: "you girls cost me more money than I will ever make back!" comments at my sister and me, turning your back on us as you go out the back door with your cigarette and whiskey.

In school I love to write, to sing, to play, write and direct theatre and my teachers encourage me. I see my path in studying arts – you make me change my application to a different school, different place and different studies as I am, in your words: "too stupid to think" that I will "ever become something special and make it anywhere," and I "will need an education to fall back on."

At 16 years of age, two months away from summer break, I get home from the daily 1-hour-each-way bus ride from school in Lysekil. It is a beautiful spring evening with the promise of a wonderful summer in the air. I am met by you having coffee with the neighbours on the stairs leading down from our front door to the lawn. Home made cookies and happy chats on the stairs.

The neighbours leave and minutes later the eyes are back.

"We don't get along. It is better if you move out. I have found an apartment close to school. You can move in after the weekend," you say while picking up the empty cups, plates and thermos to walk up the stairs and leave me sitting there.

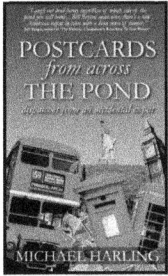

Postcards from Across the Pond

This piece by American Mike Harling, now living in England, is crammed with Scottish references and shows clearly how culture has affected his Scottish wife.

Mike's blog is www.postcardsfromacrossthepond.blogspot.com

The First, the Last and a Little in Between

My wife is half Scottish. This doesn't afflict her in many obvious ways except that she is familiar with obscure cultural references, such as First-Footing and Glasgow Kiss, and has a keen discrimination of highland single malts (her greatest compliment: "I could drink this"). As soon as we cross the border into Scotland, however, she gets in touch with her inner Celt; words like "wee" and "aye" begin slipping into her vocabulary and she starts pronouncing Loch as if she is trying to dislodge a herring bone from the back of her throat.

Your task

Write about either the person you wrote about earlier or another significant person in your life. Tell a story of an incident that happened with that person. Set the scene, describe the character, the action and add the dialogue. Write a story of 500-1000 words using the **seven steps for writing life story** and adding **SPICE**.

Seven steps to writing life stories

1. Compose
2. Review
3. Draft
4. Review
5. Polish
6. Revisit
7. Save

Spice up your life stories

- **S**pecifics
- **P**lace
- **I**ncident
- **C**haracter
- **E**motion

If you are taking the Personal Feedback Program

Please save and name your completed exercise using the YOURNAMEFIVE naming convention and email it to feedback@joparfitt.com

Now move on to complete **Lesson Six - Writing in themes**. It is recommended that you do not submit the homework for the next lesson for **personal feedback** until you have received the feedback for this **Lesson Five**.

LESSON SIX

Writing in Themes

Do specific areas of your life have their own themes? Maybe your childhood was about adventure, your teens about rejection and your twenties about friendship? You may find it is easier to write about your life by focusing on certain themes rather than looking to write about everything that happened chronologically. Many writers do this. Writing in themes makes choosing what to write about easier.

Here are some ideas for themes:

- Love
- Loss
- Release
- Exploration
- Adventure
- Pain
- Movement
- Landscape
- Family
- Empty nest
- Learning
- Breaking up
- Building
- Community
- Loneliness
- Working
- Play
- Illness
- Addiction
- Music
- Superstition
- Colour
- Shopping
- Passions
- Hates

Or you could use a more concrete theme, based around events, rituals, objects or groups.
If you want to write about your life in Holland, your themes might be:

- Water
- Landscape
- Flowers
- Food

- Buildings
- Art
- Queen's Day, the fireworks and sculpture festivals
- Friendships
- Visits
- Bars and eating out
- Shopping
- New experiences
- Language

Consider what themes arise in the country in which you now live.

Your life will have its own recurring themes. Often there will have been one main theme to each stage of your life or where you found yourself living. The things that matter to you, that you think about and that you remember most strongly will provide clues to your possible themes. In my life those themes are:

- Opportunities
- People
- Eating
- Cooking
- Entertaining
- Travel
- Writing books
- Starting again
- Working
- Saying goodbye

What are the themes in your life?

Why write in themes

Typically, writing in themes is used in columns, newsletters and blogs and can also be used to write a meaningful, revealing piece about you and your life. It allows the writer to explore a topic, find relevant stories in her life and then find meaning or resonance within those stories.

How to write in themes

When you write according to a theme, stay close to your original topic even though this may mean that you write about several related things.

For example, if you are writing about water, you could begin by writing about the lake you visited at the weekend, which then leads on to a memory of the day you learned to swim. That story could lead you to write about the day you learned to sail and that could lead to your childhood dream that sharks lurked in the water. Then that could lead to a story about the day your boat capsized and how you found that there were no sharks. A themed piece can seemingly be a bit rambling and a mix of thoughts, feelings, memories and stories; however, it does stick to a core theme.

Limbering up

Let's take a look at possible themes in your life now. Please complete the following chart, filling in details of things that may have become recurring themes and about which you could write several linked stories. I have completed this chart with a few ideas to start you off.

Who am I?

What has happened to me more than once?	What are my specialisms?	What do I or did I love doing?	How have I often felt?
Divorce In love Had children Been made redundant Moved house	Woodwork Cookery Single travel Motivating people Listening	Reading books Theatre Travel Having an adventure Cooking for friends	Alone Stressed Rejected Inspired

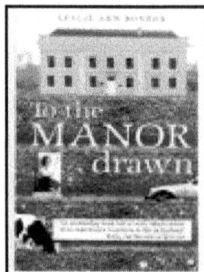

To the Manor Drawn

American Leslie-Ann Bosher has lived in England for more than 20 years, most recently in England's smallest county, Rutland. Her book shares her musings on various areas of British rural life. Each chapter has a theme.

Leslie-Ann's website is www.leslieannbosher.com

Greet and Meat

In America, the word 'barbecue' is both a verb and a noun. As a noun, 'barbecue' conjures up wonderful memories for me of family backyard gatherings where a fattening assortment of simple yet time-honoured family recipes were paraded. Aunt Betty could be counted on to prepare her famous devilled eggs and Mom could be persuaded to bring a steaming tureen of slow-cooked baked beans, with molasses, a family secret that everyone seemed to know. Potato salad tossed with onion, celery and sweet pickle and a tub of roasted, tender summer corn-on-the-cob filled out the menu. If you were lucky Ann C's version of Hoppin' John, a mixture of black-eyed peas and rice, might be on offer. Meats invariably included slabs of 5-centimeter thick, marinated prime beef and plump, white chicken breasts for the squeamish.

As afternoon drifted into evening chilled chunks of watermelon, banana pudding topped with mountains of stiff, whipped cream and homemade vanilla ice cream with warm fudge sauce made their appearance. Each of these dishes came with a tale or two as they had all been passed down through the years. It's a funny thing how old recipes can almost bring loved ones back to life. Barbecues like this just can't be exported.

Used as a verb, 'barbecue' has an entirely different meaning. As all North Carolinians know, we take the art of pig-on-the-grill cooking very seriously. In fact, the state is proudly known as the 'cradle of American barbecue'. . .

By contrast, British barbecues are often spur-of the-moment gatherings, mostly due to the unpredictability of the weather. Raised on a diet of drizzle, Brits will break out a rusty grill at the first indication of sunshine or, in some cases, snow. I think it is a ritual performed as an act of defiance against the weather gods.

A Road Traveled

Kim Brice, an American, wrote the following, on love.

There have been 10 of them I think. I love them all I suppose in one way or another. They all took me to various parts of the world. That was the plus. If the relationships didn't work out, at least I had learned a new language, tasted new foods and met interesting characters along the way.

1977.

Name: Hugo Thørning.
Origin: Langå, Denmark.
He lived in: Langå, Denmark.
I lived in: Manhattan, New York.

Most memorable: he is the first teacher who saw me as somebody, an 11 year old with valuable thoughts, concerns and feelings.

Lasted: six lessons or 12 hours and a crush.

1979.

Name: Felix Partow.
Origin: Iran.
He lived in: Manhattan, New York.
I lived in: Manhattan, New York.

Most memorable: he dared me to dance a slow dance. I dared back. It was the first time my heart beat really fast for someone else. I thought I might faint.

Lasted: two slow dances and three years' worth of fleeting stares.

1982.

Name: Luca Dussi.
Origin: Rahway, New Jersey.
He lived in: Milan, Italy.
I lived in: Manhattan, New York.

Most memorable: it was the real thing: pure, young love, so deep it hurt.

Lasted: five years, two months and 350 letters.

1990.

Name: Panivong.
Origin: Laos.
He lived in: Princeton, NJ.
I lived in: Manhattan, New York.

Most memorable: he was my manager at the Carvel Ice Cream store, my first job ever. He felt like home.

Lasted: two summer months and 325 ice cream cones.

1990.

Name: Mark Calafatello.
Origin: Staten Island, New York.
He lived in: Oneanta, New York.
I lived in: Manhattan, New York.

Most memorable: one interminable kiss, it made my lips sore.

Lasted: three weekends and a Supertramp concert.

1985.

Name: Chris Minot.
Origin: Don't know.
He lived in: Nairobi, Kenya.
I lived in: Nairobi, Kenya.

Most memorable: it's the first time I ever wanted to protect someone from himself.

Lasted: four months and six hours, most of it in my head

1987.

Name: Can't remember.
Origin: Lahore, Pakistan.
Living in: Amherst, Massachusetts.
I lived in: Northampton, Massachusetts.

Most memorable: he had arranged marriage written all over his face.

Lasted: three hours, one movie and the time it takes to have a fantasy about wearing a red wedding sari.

1995.

Name: Fabio Castillo.

Origin: Bogotá, Colombia.
Living in: Port-au-Prince, Haiti.
I lived in: Port-au-Prince, Haiti.

Most memorable: he hurt me.

Lasted: two years, three continents and two therapy sessions.

1996.

Name: Jesper Højberg.
Origin: Copenhagen, Denmark.
Living in: Harare, Zimbabwe.
I lived in: Johannesburg, South Africa.

Most memorable: I felt happy and free enough to believe I was in love and for good.

Lasted: eight months, two flights and 40 phone calls.

1998.

Name: Kees Hommes.
Origin: Assen, Netherlands.
Living in: Johannesburg, South Africa.
I lived in: Johannesburg, South Africa.

Most memorable: he's the glove that fits and we regularly laugh each other to tears.

Lasted: nine years (and still going) and thousands of "I love yous".

Moments

Celeste Maguire, wrote on the theme of Moments. Notice how she uses phrases that evoke much more than would a dialogue between two people or a story.

There are moments in your life when in a few seconds everything changes. Life as you know it will never be the same. The worst sentence in the world is: "Are you sitting down, I have something to tell you." Time stands still. An eternity happens in those few seconds before the words are spoken.

Moments.

"Dad has lung cancer."
"There's been an accident."
"Mom died early this morning."
"I'm sorry, we've lost everything."

Breathtakingly painful moments that bring you to your knees.

And then there are the moments that bring so much joy, your heart seems to burst with happiness. You want to run and jump and hug the world.

"The test is positive, you are pregnant."
"I love you, will you marry me?"
"It's a boy!"
"Mom, the twins were born this morning and they're both healthy."

Moments.

Such short sentences that carry so much power. Signposts pointing to the new direction life will take. A few seconds in time contain the power of a lifetime.

A Life With a Theme

Debbie Beasley-Suffolk, from England, wrote the following about music. See how introspective she is and how she combines flashback to her childhood with a sense of place.

When you hit forty, a strange sensation comes over you. Perhaps it's because the older generation is fading away and childhood seeps further into the background of life's unfolding portrait, but somewhere in the forties, one finds oneself in an increasingly reflective frame of mind. Perhaps it has crept upon the psyche like the morning mist over the dew dripped grass, or slapped the spirit suddenly as the thunderbolt of a summer storm that heralds the abrupt end to a balmy evening.

Thoughts race through the mind. Am I more than half way through my life? What have I done with it? What haven't I done with it? Contemplation of what has preceded is healthy: it helps form decisions for the future.

How many of us can say that our lives so far have been full and well used? And how many of us can see a common thread running through this existence to date, that has shaped us thus far and gives potential definition for the time to come? Do you have a unifying motif in your life?

I am most definitely a themed person. My life always has and, I hope, always will revolve around music. Music is work, rest and play for me. As the saying goes, I live and breathe it.

There isn't a time when I don't recall music being around me and in my home. My father

was, amongst other things, a drummer in a four-piece dance band who played every weekend of my childhood in dance halls around the local district of our northeast England home. Dad practised new rhythms on his beautiful pearlescent blue drum kit in the main bedroom of our small miner's cottage so often that we children ceased to notice it and would quite easily fall asleep at night during his practice sessions.

The memory of my conscious decision to make music myself is as fresh as ever. I was five years old and one autumnal evening Dad was playing our old German upright piano in the front room of our cottage as he did regularly for entertainment and to 'keep his hand in'. The fire was burning invitingly in the grate but I sat on the floor in the opposite corner beside the piano's carved ornamental columns, as always, to watch Dad's feet on the pedals and listen to the melodies above my head. This time something new happened. I watched his hands instead. Dad was playing the 'Black and White Rag' by Scott Joplin. It was a popular piece at that time as it was used as the title music for a TV snooker programme called 'Pot Black'. As his right hand whizzed up and down the keys with the intricate melody and the left hand bounced with the pulsating jazz rhythm, I was transfixed. Forgetting the feet, I had made the connection where the wonderful sounds above my head were produced. How much more exciting the hands were! This is it. This is what I want to do, I thought.

And so this was the beginning of a wonderful, enriching, endless world of hard work and enjoyment, of reward and disappointment, of high adrenalin and exhaustion, of hopes and fears, of . . . everything! If anyone wants to experience the full gamut of human emotion then they can do no better than to become a musician. It won't let you down. Oh. And just to let you know, I've had a relatively good career on the piano but I've not yet learnt the 'Black and White Rag': I'm hopeless at jazz.

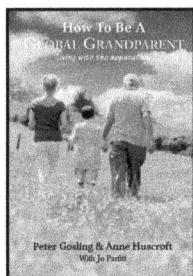

How to be a Global Grandparent

This extract, by Peter Gosling, has also been published in two separate magazines as a humorous column. It uses exaggeration and understatement to make it funny. By the way, Peter is my father.

You can find out more about this book at www.theglobalgrandparent.com

Lists

"I'm going to get married," our daughter suddenly announced.

Sighs of relief all round. We thought he was never going to ask her.

"And we're going to live abroad."

"Where?" we asked, our jaws dropping.

"It's in the Gulf," she explained. "Look, I'll show you."

She opened the atlas and pointed to a place that was a black dot in the middle of a vast sandy-coloured area. It seemed one heck of a way from England.

"You'll be able to visit us," she said seeing that our faces had assumed a look of terror at the thought of our little girl being trapped in an oasis surrounded by camels.

"It's really quite civilised," she explained patiently. "They have shops, proper houses and an airport."

And so it was that a few months after the frantic arrangements for the wedding and the tearful farewells, the call came.

"We've got a nice flat and there's a spare room for you. Do come, you'll love it. And by the way, could you bring . . . ?"

That was the start of the lists that were going to dominate our lives for the next few years. At first it was just a few of the wedding presents that had taken up residence in our garage. Oh, and could we possibly cram some of her favourite tea in our case, and a couple of pork pies (impossible to get out there) and her Cliff Richard tapes.

Your task

Write about a theme in your life or the life of another person. Write a story of 500-1000 words using the **seven steps for writing life story** and adding **SPICE**.

Seven steps to writing life stories

1. Compose
2. Review
3. Draft
4. Review
5. Polish
6. Revisit
7. Save

Spice up your life stories

- **S**pecifics
- **P**lace
- **I**ncident
- **C**haracter
- **E**motion

If you are taking the Personal Feedback Program

Please save and name your completed exercise using the YOURNAMESIX naming convention and email it to feedback@joparfitt.com

Now move on to complete **Lesson Seven - Writing humour**. It is recommended that you do not submit the homework for the next lesson for **personal feedback** until you have received the feedback for this **Lesson Six**.

LESSON SEVEN

Writing humour

In this lesson we are going to learn to write about the funny things that happen in our lives, the events you find yourself telling again and again at dinner parties or in the pub.

The trouble with writing humour is that something that makes you laugh uproariously when you tell the story live, is much harder to write down. When you share a story with people who know the characters involved, or recognise the situation, it is more likely to raise a laugh than when the same story is read by a complete stranger.

This lesson will help you to find your writing funny bone. It will help you to decide which stories will work in writing and which will not.

Humour is...

- Seeing the funny side of a difficult situation

- Homing in on the way someone goes through hell to achieve a goal

- Highlighting the romantic ideal and contrasting it with the less than pleasant reality

- Over-statement

- Laughing with rather than at your characters

- Giving characters a quirk or annoying habit

- Wordplay
  - Puns that deliberately exploit ambiguity between similar sounding words

- Slapstick that is funny
  - Exaggerated physical violence or accident that is highly unlikely to happen in real life

- Irony that is funny
  - To benefit from an unlikely situation

- Sarcasm that is funny
  - Saying one thing when you mean the opposite – usually spoken

- Parody that is funny
  - The humorous imitation of someone or something. Also known as spoof or lampoon

- Ridicule and abuse/satire
  - Vices, madness, shortcomings are held up for scrutiny and ridicule, often with the goal of making someone change his ways

- The sense of the absurd
- Reversion of the logical to the illogical
- The comedy of the individual/eccentricity

What's funny?

Funny stories work when shared with groups or people or readers who can empathise with the situation.

I usually run live writing workshops in Holland. Houses are notoriously smaller than elsewhere, and when one student began to talk about her new doll-sized kitchen with the question: "Do the Dutch cook?" everyone fell about laughing. She did not need to explain how small the kitchen was, we knew.

When stand-up comedian Michael McIntyre talks about the weird items that men keep in their 'man drawer', such as foreign coins, spent batteries and radiator bleeding keys, everyone laughs because either they are male and also have one of these drawers, or they are female and know someone with just such a drawer.

Don't forget that laughing and crying both include tears and both are closer than you think. You know the phrase: 'if I didn't laugh I'd cry'. Laughter can come from 'there but by the grace of God go I' incidents.

What we do not understand we fear, and if we fear we find a space to laugh in. Let's take a look at the following example:

Situation: a mother is doing the food shopping in the foreign town to which she has just moved. She does not speak the language and does not know her way around.

Humour can be found in:

- **Her panic**
- **Her uselessness at the language**
- **Her fear**
- **The mistakes she makes**
- **The way she pretends to her husband or kids or mother, if they call, that she's fine.**
- **The silly things she does to make herself understood**
- **Her lack of knowledge**
- **Her inability to do something that should be normal**
- **The 'there but for the grace of God go I' element**
- **The fact that we can empathise**

How to write humour

Everyone likes to laugh, but not everyone knows how to make people laugh. Being able to write humour, whether fiction or non-fiction, is a talent that can be sharpened by following a few simple steps.

1. Be observant
People find situations that they can relate to funny. This is why so many stand-up comedians begin their jokes with, "Have you ever noticed . . . ?" or "Why is it that . . . ?" Don't invent situations, just keep your eyes open and funny situations will make themselves known to you.

2. Humour is pain
People find humour in the suffering of others. Sure, it can be cruel, but what's funnier: someone walking down the road and falling down a manhole or someone walking down the road and finding a dropped wallet?

3. Exaggerate the negative
It's cruel, but it's easier to find humour in something bad than something good. See how humorous columnist, Jeremy Clarkson focuses on the bad things in the cars he writes about. Exaggerate numbers. Say there were 5,000 people in the queue in front of you. That you were in a traffic jam for a week.

4. Find exaggerated situations
Writing about an event from your everyday life, like planning your family's supper, might not be very funny, but having the school basketball team turn up for dinner when all you have in the house is a tin of tomatoes and some monkfish, can be funny.

5. Look for the bizarre
Have you ever taken a bus journey with a group of footballers dressed in drag? Or stood behind someone dressed as a pumpkin in the supermarket queue? Been stopped by the police on the day you had dashed to the shops in your pyjamas?

6. Be specific
For some reason it is funnier if you name things like cars or brands rather than use the generic term. Saying that "I found a feather in my Fanta" or that "I got mud all over my Manolos" is much funnier than "I found a feather in my fizzy orange" or "I got mud on my shoes". If you can use a word that rhymes, assonates, alliterates or is just plain absurd then all the better. Like in the extract below, when Sue's cookbook fell off the shelf she says "Delia Smith's Christmas flopped down in my flapjack". Perhaps it wasn't that book at all and perhaps it really fell into her soup, but using those words made it funnier.

7. Pretend you are telling a joke
Jokes have a set-up and punch line, and the punch line should not be delivered too early. If you can set the joke up and build the tension even better.

8. Test it out

David Sedaris reads his essays aloud first of all before he commits the final draft to paper. If sections make people laugh he keeps them, if not, he bins them.

9. Focus on normality

Write about everyday things that everyone can relate to. Sleeping, eating, shopping, working, having children. Humour can be based on truth.

10. Laugh at yourself

Be self-deprecating. Show yourself as the bumbling victim. Overplay your stupidity. Remember how the court jester was also called the 'fool'.

Limbering up

Think of a funny situation that you often share with your friends. Look back at the chart, above. Now, let's find the humour . . .

_____

Describe the situation, briefly.

_____

Set up the story. What had led up to this?

_____

Set the scene. Describe the setting. Maybe it will contrast the event or match it perfectly.

_____

Where is the humour to be found?

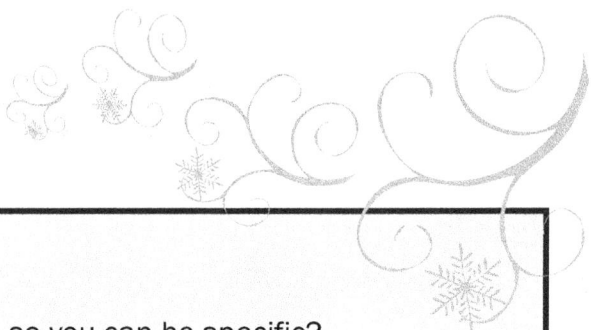

What brand names could you mention so you can be specific?

_____

How can you be self-deprecating?

_____

What could you exaggerate?

_____

What is absurd about this situation?

_____

What is funny about the characters involved? Do they have a quirk?
Do they dress oddly or speak oddly?

_____

What fundamental truth do you write about here that will resonate
with readers?

_____

What is excruciating or painful about this situation?

Extract – Forced to Fly. This piece is by Sue Ventris

This includes a sense of the absurd and the fact that we can empathise with this everyday situation. It begins with 'picture this' and indeed we can. There is much exaggeration. Notice how there are specifics like Sainsbury's pie, Crunchie and Fisher Price. Much of it may not be true, but that adds to the fun.

The Visitors from Hell

Picture this . . . The perfect visitors from back home arrive at your expatriate door. They're laden with bulging suitcases crammed with jars of Marmite, freezer food from Marks and Spencer and catering packs of Crunchie bars. They stagger beneath the weight of boxes containing a Fisher Price kitchen and a full size trampoline. In their hand luggage they've gamely smuggled six litres of spirits, then declare a thirst for tap water.

You love these visitors. They have their own hire car, and use it. They depart early each morning on sightseeing trips, returning at nightfall just in time to help the children with their homework. Their favourite meal is beans on toast, which they cook themselves. They're fluent in the local language and translate your awkward documents for you. They stay no longer than 48 hours.

These visitors are not your relatives.

Your relatives arrive with suitcases crammed with medications and a vast wardrobe for themselves, catering for all eventualities from Arctic snowstorms to blistering heat. They forget the duty free, then head straight for your gin bottle. You feel a brief flurry of excitement at the sight of a Sainsbury's pie, but it's turkey and ham and you've been vegetarian for years.

Once on foreign soil, your parents lose all power of independent movement. One of these days they'll start following you into the bathroom. They never hire a car, or if they do, they're too nervous to drive it. They lie in bed until 10 o'clock while you sort out the kids and do the school run. They then arise, raring to go. Each day they expect you to take them on excursions that leave you perpetually exhausted. Once home after these jaunts, their energy deserts them, and they flop into an armchair while you cook the evening meal.

I Was Only Trying to Help

Peter Gosling had this piece published in Emirates Man magazine, Dubai. Much of the humour here comes from the fact that we can empathise. It is exaggerated. There is self-deprecation of the author and he tells a number of stories that all illustrate his clumsiness.

That great humorous writer, schoolmaster, raconteur and Welsh wit, the late Gwyn Thomas, once wrote a story in which the main character was the owner of a hotdog stall. It told how this unfortunate person was absentmindedly picking up a sliced roll ready for the next customer. His index finger slipped into the slit and without further thought he covered the unfortunate digit with ketchup and took a bite! I am accident prone in this way, much to the annoyance and occasional amusement of my family. If there is drink to be carried it inevitably spills, however careful I am. If I wear the white trousers that I consider the height of elegance, they attract curry like a magnet. If I go through a doorway where the handles are of the lever type I am sure to get one of them caught in the sleeve of my jacket thus bringing me to a premature and undignified halt. Mornings are the worst time for this type of problem, when the loop of the belt of my dressing gown has a habit of getting wound round the first protruding knob or handle as I make my way downstairs.

We have some good friends, still, who have never forgotten that on leaving their house one day I walked straight into one of their new rose bushes and both I and the bush ended up horizontal.

If I go out to a meal it always seems that after the table has been cleared my place is clearly marked by a circle of crumbs and a red wine stain. So I have recently got into the habit of surreptitiously trying to brush the offending mess on to the floor, only it usually gets on to my trousers and jacket front producing a confetti-like shower when I finally stand up to go.

My best trick happens if I have to visit the bathroom during a meal. It always seems to be my lot to eat in places where the water pressure is abnormally high. The slightest turn of the tap causes a Niagara of water to spurt out all over my trousers. Panic-stricken I try to dry the offending drops. Hot air driers are too high off the ground to be of any effect, and towels are of little use. So I return to my place with knees bent and pressed together in a vain attempt to cover up the embarrassing dampness.

"Sorry I was so long, the roller towel . . . looking for the soap . . ." My excuses only make it worse.

Washing up is full of traps for the likes of me although I tend these days to be allowed to attempt such a thing only when the glasses are quite thick and the bone china service is not in use. Crashing the crystal glass against the taps is not something I care to do very often. I well remember drying a champagne glass and twisting the stem off in my enthusiasm. The glass was a wedding present belonging to the friends I was visiting and we were celebrating their return from honeymoon. They were really very nice about it.

A golfing friend of mine put his finger on it, when he heard that I was taking lessons in the game.

"The trouble with you," he said, "is that you lack coordination!"

He could well be right. I did once manage to lose a ball before I had even reached the first tee. It is quite possible that I have some sort of mental block when it comes to spatial

concepts, which proved to be quite a problem when I used to teach mathematics. Visualising things in three dimensions has always been difficult. I appear not to have the ability to, for example, visualise what a room or a garden will look like after some feature has been altered. Draw me a picture and I've got it, otherwise I am quite at a loss.

I've often noticed that I have difficulty not in making choices, but rather in carrying them out. If I have the choice of two tapes to play I have little difficulty in making up my mind. However, I often end up by putting the wrong tape into the machine. If I am helping prepare vegetables for the freezer I find that often the peas get thrown away while I place the pods carefully in the bowl. It could be that I'm a hurrier not a worrier. I am usually thinking about several things at once and somehow the thoughts get confused. Again, returning to my days as a mathematician, I always used to say that I had to do each problem twice, once to get it wrong and a second time to get it right!

When I was preparing this piece I found that I couldn't think of a suitable tag line to end it. You know, the clever twist at the end. The bon mot that makes everyone think: That's a clever piece of writing! But I was lost for an idea so I went to have my lunch, opened a packet of bread buns, extracted one and was just on the point of throwing it into the waste bin and buttering the packet when I realised what I was doing.

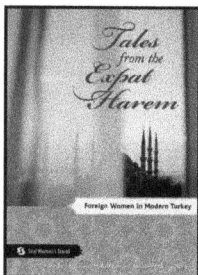

Extract – Tales from the Expat Harem. This piece is by Maria Yarborough Orhon

The element of surprise makes this extract funny. The author also uses exaggeration and overstatement. The dialogue is well-crafted and is accompanied by action.

You can find this book at www.expatharem.com

A Mother's Charms

"Where is your belly button?" my Turkish boyfriend Ibrahim asked me one night in the 1970s as I sipped white wine at a fish restaurant beside the Bosphorus.

"Pardon me?" I sputtered, hoping I hadn't dribbled on my silk blouse.

"Your belly button. Where is it?"

"Oh Ibo, for goodness sake, it's here, of course," I snapped back, pointing vaguely toward my middle, annoyed that he was being so silly.

"No, no, I mean the part that falls off later," he went on.

"Oh. You mean the umbilical cord," I mumbled, glancing around to see if anyone was overhearing this oddly intimate exchange. "I don't know. They probably threw it out a the hospital or something." As I spoke, I realised I had no idea what Americans did with a newborn's dried umbilical stem.

I rearranged my napkin daintily in my lap, wondering where this strange conversation was going. "So, where's yours, anyway?" I said, deciding to put the ball back in his court.

"My mother has it, safely tucked away. You're supposed to keep it as a kind of amulet to ward off harmful things. Too bad about yours," he said, cutting into his salmon.

I sat there staring at my sautéed shrimp, feeling slightly squeamish. I'd known Ibo for

four years and had always thought of him as being very modern
and European. Certainly in Turkey, his native land and my home on
and off for nearly a decade, there were superstitions, particularly the fear of
something called the 'evil eye'.

Extract – Forced to Fly. This piece is by Sue Valentine

It was only putting up a shelf, but achieving this seemed impossible in this piece about an absurd situation. The carpenters are presented as hapless and satire is used to ridicule them. The author is not blameless, as she seems to have rather a problem with kettle floods and cookery books anyway. Again, we can empathise. Alliteration, in the form of 'sliding sideways' and 'flopped down into my flapjack' adds to the humour. Notice the use of a book title makes it funnier. Like, Visitors from Hell, above, this appeared in an anthology.

The Carpenter Came to Call

The recipe books were too numerous for the space they held on the counter, somewhere between the cooker and the sink. The books had been preventing me from serving up a meal onto four plates for several weeks and had recently acquired the habit of sliding sideways like dominoes in the wake of regular kettle floods. I needed a shelf. Time, then, to call a carpenter. Easy, you would think. But I live in a Middle Eastern country where the workmen tend to be paid little and are rarely fluent in English. A place where houses are all rented and we are told that all communication with the landlord must come from a male.

So, I asked my husband to ask the maintenance man to ask the carpenter to telephone and make an appointment.

The following day the carpenter called round at the house himself unannounced.
I was out, of course.

"When did he say he would come back?" I asked Roti, our housegirl.

"He didn't say, ma'am."

Oh well, start again. This time I asked my husband to ask the maintenance man for the carpenter's telephone number.

I broke with convention and called the carpenter myself. He arrived at the appointed time.

I gave him a drawing and explained what was required – a fatal mistake. Never try to explain when there is a language barrier. It just gives you a false sense of security because you invariably receive smiles and nods in reply, which unfortunately do not mean "yes", but instead "I am very friendly and willing and would like to please you but don't understand a word you are saying."

The carpenter took out his retractable tape measure and measured. Twice. He failed to write anything down.

I asked him if he fully understood. Yes, you've guessed it, he nodded and smiled and said, "yes madam."

Time passed. The pages of my cookery books were crinkled and glued together from a

mixture of water and spilled gravy. I asked my husband to call the maintenance man who would, in turn, call the carpenter. Nothing. I asked my husband to call the carpenter. Still nothing. In the end I called the carpenter myself. I called the maintenance man myself. In time the carpenter did indeed reappear with the shelf, sorry that is not strictly true: he returned with a shelf. It was the correct length – an amazing feat when you consider he had only to rely on his memory. It was round about the right width too – nothing short of a miracle. But the wood was rough and unpainted and there was not a bracket in sight.

I asked about the supports of course. I pointed at my copy of the original drawing, which clearly showed brackets.

"Coming, madam," he replied and nodded and smiled some more.

I asked about the rough wood.

"We are painting, madam," he assured.

True to his word, later that day, the carpenter's friend and his assistant arrived with a tin of paint. Three men with wide brushes painted my narrow shelf, then stood it on its wet end in the middle of my patio and went away.

Three days later they returned triumphantly with the supports. I think they wanted to impress me for they had already been painted. A different colour.

Eventually, the damage done to the paintwork, which had been caused by the less than clean concrete on which it had stood, was repaired. They even corrected the discrepancy in the colour. They attached it to the wall using the brackets. At just the second attempt it was straight – once I had suggested they borrow our spirit level.

A year later, the shelf still stands. But today, when Delia Smith's Christmas flopped down into my flapjack, I came to the stark realisation that my cookery books have been at it again. They have been multiplying without my consent. I guess it's time to get my husband to call the maintenance man to call that carpenter again. Or maybe I'll do it myself this time?

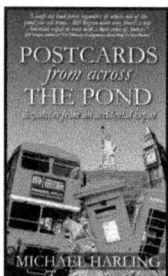

Extract – Postcards from Across the Pond by Mike Harling

Exaggeration, satire and comedic observation of the absurd make this a funny piece about Europe as seen through the eyes of American, Mike Harling.

Mike's blog is at www.postcardsfromacrossthepond.blogspot.com

Peek-A-Boob Telly

Something happened last night that reminded me why I love the Brits. But to understand, I'm afraid we're going to have to undergo a cultural primer.

On the other side of the Atlantic Ocean is a largish land mass known as Europe – you might recall this from your high school geography class. Europe is made up of a baker's dozen of little countries that periodically set about fighting one another, forcing the US to step in and sort things out. England is technically part of Europe, but it's not attached – there is this channel thing between the European mainland and England itself, which keeps England from being totally European and more like America, only smaller.

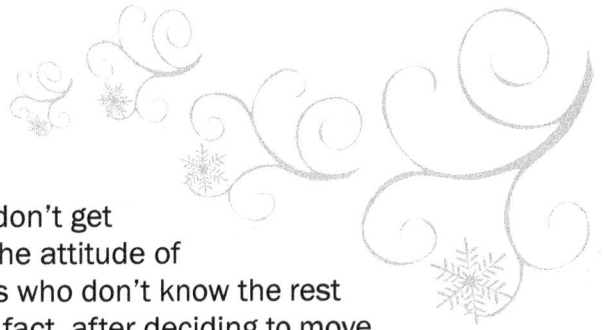

This is really all you need to know for now. And don't get me wrong, I didn't write the previous paragraphs with the attitude of "I'm the worldly traveller and you are all ugly Americans who don't know the rest of the world exists." I didn't know any of that, either. In fact, after deciding to move here I had to look at a map to find out where London was (I thought it was much closer to Scotland).

Anyway, after the last big war, the countries decided they needed to work together to establish a peaceful union. The best way to accomplish this, they agreed, was to hold an international song contest. (No, I am not making this up. *The Eurovision Song Contest* – which this article is about – pre-dates the formation of the European Economic Community, forerunner of the European Union, by two years. The EU is a group of countries that periodically sends representatives to Brussels to make silly laws and print money no one likes. They do have a nifty flag though.)

The Eurovision Song Contest (which, incidentally, is much more popular than the EU) is held each year in May. It's sort of a cross between a poor-man's Las Vegas extravaganza and a 'battle of the bands' competition and features the type of earnest yet annoying talent you normally associate with teenagers and garages; you know, the ones you wish would go out and smoke dope or vandalize something just so you can get some peace and quiet. The whole affair is so hopelessly tacky it is impossible not to watch it.

Your task

Take a funny story from your life and write about it now. Write a story of 500-1000 words using the **seven steps for writing life story** and adding **SPICE**.

Seven steps to writing life stories

1. Compose
2. Review
3. Draft
4. Review
5. Polish
6. Revisit
7. Save

Spice up your life stories

- **S**pecifics
- **P**lace
- **I**ncident
- **C**haracter
- **E**motion

If you are taking the Personal Feedback Program

Please save and name your completed exercise using the YOURNAMESEVEN naming convention and email it to feedback@joparfitt.com

Now move on to complete **Lesson Eight - Writing in stories**. It is recommended that you do not submit the homework for the next lesson for **personal feedback** until you have received the feedback for this **Lesson Seven.**

LESSON EIGHT

Writing in stories

The best non-fictional accounts read like fiction. Fictional stories have both plot and pace, and the reader keeps turning pages because he wants to discover what happens next. This lesson will show you how to give your life stories qualities that make them compelling to read. Stories with a beginning, middle and end.

Often a story will have some kind of a journey. This may be a physical journey where you move from one place to another, even if that journey is just down the road to the shops. Or it can be an emotional journey, when the reader watches you, or the character you write about moves from one state to another, from panic to peace, for example.

In a good story something happens and something changes as a result, however small that change. The change may be in your opinion of something or someone, or you may learn something new, have an insight or a beneficial encounter. You may become enriched, enlightened or amused. But, by and large, something will happen. It is your job as the storyteller to try and make your piece as interesting and compelling as a piece of fiction.

As I said earlier, the best stories will not only include all the elements of SPICE, but also a plot, with a beginning, middle and end.

The narrative should reflect the content. So if you are describing a languid, lazy day you can use long sentences. But a car chase would benefit from short sentences.

A story has the following:

- Plot
- Character
- Dialogue
- Pace
- Setting and sense of place
- Insight or resonance
- Emotion

In order to create a story you need to:

- Pay attention as things happen
- Notice the details
- Notice the way things make you feel
- Notice the insights that come to you
- Listen to what people say and how they say it

Pay attention

You were introduced to the importance of paying attention in Lesson Two, Letting it Flow. This skill is very important if you want to be a good storyteller. By learning to pay attention properly to what is going on, you see more and find more insights.

The more you practise the easier it becomes . . . the more you notice and . . . the more you remember . . . and you write a rich and varied journal, filled with insights.

The more disciplined you are about writing a journal – you WILL write every night before bed, when you get home from work, when the children leave for school or every Saturday morning at 11, or whatever – the more you will start to notice things that you will put in your journal during the day. And this is the trick. Looking back and trying to remember does not work half so well as noticing something at the time it takes place. Train yourself to notice things and then file the good bits away in your memory ready for your journal. Making a conscious effort to remember something later sets the thought/feeling/insight in stone so it is easier to recall later.
Can you remember what your family was wearing on Christmas Day? Or what the weather was like. Who can remember what they had for supper on Sunday night? I can't. But if it was important I made a mental note at the time and then wrote about it in my journal later.

I've been journaling since I was 11. And I've made my living as a writer since I was in my early twenties, so I'm practised at this. I have taught myself to notice things as they happen.

Some tips to help you pay attention

- Be in the moment, in the zone
- Stop for a moment and notice what is happening and how you feel
- Be quiet
- Meditate

The story-writing process

What follows is a story I wrote last year. After you read it I will explain how the story evolved.

Wake up and smell the coffee

It all began with a cup of coffee . . .

It's taken us two years but we have finally given in and bought a Nespresso coffee machine. At first I was dead against it. Regardless of the beauty of those little pods of coffee. Despite how easy the machine was to use and clean. Despite the €50 discount they offer at this time of year and regardless of the fact that it makes the best coffee I have tasted, I refused to succumb because I was convinced it was a scam. How could a company lure you into buying a coffee machine and then force you to keep on buying its own overpriced pods of coffee for evermore? It was a travesty. A downright con trick. There was no way I was going to fall for that one.
     But last week we were invited to dinner with friends and they offered us a Nespresso after the meal. They were delighted with their own machine and shared the story of their

conversion away from Senseo and the coffee 'pad' to the coffee 'pod'. Our friends gave us a choice of 12 varieties of coffee, including three types of decaffeinated. It seemed Mr Nespresso had thought of everything. He'd even given the coffees a clever upmarket feel by dressing them up with Italian names that made you think of piazzas, opera and Michelangelo.

A couple of days later, we noticed that they were giving away free tastings of Nespresso in a local department store. Deciding it couldn't hurt to try it just once more, and, footsore from a few hours in the sales, we joined the queue at the coffee bar. While we waited, we watched in awe the volume of customers who stood in line at two separate counters to buy their supplies of coffee pods. Who, in their right mind, I thought, would buy a coffee machine that only used its own brand coffee, and then have to make a special effort to buy more each time it ran out? I mean, the pods aren't even available in supermarkets!

But, half an hour later we joined that queue to buy our first machine and a supply of coffee pods and became part of the Nespresso club, which meant that we were given a username and a beautiful ring bound file of instructions and one of those neat presentation boxes that make the coffee pods look luxurious, like expensive chocolates. We handed over the credit card.

"Why is this making me feel glad to be parting with my cash?" said my husband, Ian, with a smile. "What is it about this experience that makes everyone so incredibly happy?"

Perhaps it is the buzz of the caffeine, which, it has been proved, puts people in a buying mood? Or perhaps there is something alluring about the gem-like pods, so artfully displayed? Why is Nespresso such a raging success? What I do know is that anyone with something to sell has much to learn from the people who used to be known for their frankly unexceptional instant coffee.

That evening, over supper, I shared my insights with my family.

"What else can you think of then, that once you buy it, forces you to keep on buying supplies from the same people?" I asked.

"A printer?" suggested my husband.

"Yes," I said, with some hesitation, knowing that you could buy ink from cheaper sources than the original HP or Epson manufacturer, and you could even get them refilled at a copy shop, so maybe it didn't quite count.

"A car?" suggested my son. "You have to keep filling a car up with petrol once you buy it."

Again, I was not sure. When you bought a car from Ford, say, you did not have to return to Ford to buy your petrol. Still, I was excited by my theory and pondered it as I buzzed gently from my third cappuccino of the day, decaffeinated this time.

Three days later, as my son selected a gold pod of Volluto from the sleek black box to have a much-needed espresso that would jolt him into action on the first day of term, we got our answer.

"Heroin," he said. "It's just like being hooked on heroin."

I was stunned into silence. He was right.

This is how my story evolved

- I went to dinner at a friend's house and at the end of the meal was offered a cup of coffee. Right away I noticed the beauty of the coffee pods and variety of coffee and made a mental note.

- A couple of days later, we decided to buy a Nespresso.

- Went to the department store and saw you could test the coffee there and then. I noticed the queue, the display and realised this was worth noticing. At the time I recognised that this was an entrepreneur's dream so paid extra special attention while we made our decision and how it felt as we bought it and what my husband said to me as we did so. I wrote about all that in my journal that evening.

- The next morning over breakfast I told the children how excited I was by the Nespresso phenomenon and asked them for ideas knowing I may use them in my story.

- I wrote my story.

- A couple of days later my son told me about his heroin idea.

- I rewrote my ending.

- It took a little over a week, but I kept on paying attention until I had my ending.

Now it's your turn.

Limbering up

Often the best examples of complete stories are those that you find yourself telling at dinner parties or with old friends. Typically these stories will have a beginning, middle and end as well as a crisis resolved or funny ending.

Make a note here of the stories you often find yourself telling. Make a list.

My stories

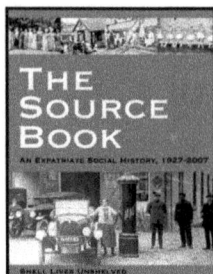

Extract – The Sourcebook, compiled by The Expatriate Archive Centre, PS, Venezuela, 1995; 0509/473

A foreign woman needs to buy a bra in a country where she does not speak the language and a crowd gathers as she and her three male helpers assist with the embarrassing purchase. It is a complete story, beginning as it does with a crisis and leading to its resolution. The situation is humorous.

Find out more about the archive at www.xpatarchive.com

Buying a bra

One morning, before we went to work, my wife washed her bra and knickers and spread them out on the balcony of our room to dry. When we returned in the evening we found that the wind had got up and had blown the bra off the balcony. This caused some consternation as she had only brought two bras with her.

Savala, the driver, was consulted and he said, "Of course. I know just the place. We will go there tomorrow after work."

Work the next day finished about 5pm so we set off for the bra shop in Puerto Cabello. Savala was the navigator, Carlos was the interpreter, my wife was the customer and I was there solely to pay the bill. The shop, which was in a narrow street in the old part of the town, was about eight feet wide and ten feet deep. It was absolutely crammed with all sorts of female undergarments.

The proprietress was somewhat taken aback by three men and one woman filling the shop. Anyway, the pantomime opened by Savala explaining that he had brought Madam here because he knew it was a good shop selling only the best. I expect he was hoping for a commission on the business he had brought in. Carlos then explained what was required, referring frequently to my wife for details and specifications. Many bras were produced, and finally my wife was persuaded to try one on, fortunately in the 'fitting room' behind the counter. This went on three or four times and by now a small crowd had gathered outside the shop to see what was going on.

Eventually, a new bra was purchased, much to the amusement of the audience, and to the relief of Carlos. Savala thoroughly enjoyed the whole episode.

The moral of this story is: 'if you cannot speak the language, always take three bras with you, especially in South America.'

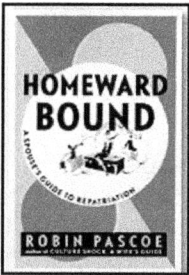

Extract – Homeward Bound
by Robin Pascoe

Canadian Robin Pascoe is the author of several books for expatriates. Here is the story of her meltdown in a telephone store. There is a crisis, its conclusion, humour and insight.

More of Robin's writing can be found at www.expatexpert.com

Buying a smart phone

I wandered around the telephone showroom to check out the latest in phone décor and function as I waited for my number to be called. My eyes glazed over at the sheer magnitude of the selection. Perched atop pedestals, sophisticated track lighting showcasing them like works of futuristic fine art, some telephones boasted features that quite frankly baffled me.

When I was finally called to the customer wicket, my problem turned out not to be with the questions I had jotted down to ask, but with the answers offered by the clerk who had the misfortune to have me as a customer that day. Most of her answers were incomprehensible. It was like being abroad again and knowing little bits of the local language, proudly using them with shopkeepers only to get hit in the face by a stream of words that made absolutely no sense. Overseas, I always received a smile for my efforts. There were no smiles for me on this day as I politely inquired how to go about setting up separate lines for our phone, fax and Internet.

Barely looking up from paperwork generated by the previous customer, the phone bureaucrat informed me I would likely require a smart phone for the purpose I had in mind.

"Yes," I answered politely, thinking of the phone art around me. "I would like it to look smart."

"No," said the woman in a voice reserved for children and newcomers to Canada who don't yet speak English, "Not a phone that looks smart. One that acts smart."

"Could you please explain that again?" Tears, an almost daily occurrence at that time, were waiting to pounce behind eyeballs still spinning from my showroom tour. At the same time, self-loathing was working its way into my system. I couldn't believe I was getting so agitated over a stupid telephone.

Her explanation was technical drivel to me. Did I care that telephone lines could magically be split in two and the phone would automatically flip a switch if the caller was in fact a caller or a fax machine, or indeed a long distance caller using a fax machine? My heart started to race and knees to wobble. A panic attack could no longer patiently wait on hold. The clerk began drawing diagrams on the back of an envelope. I became more confused and knew hostility was threatening to overload my emotional switchboard.

Too late. A switch flipped. My panic tuned to anger and tears of frustration burst from my eyes. I irrationally decided that blame for this debacle must definitely be assigned to my husband. Why wasn't he here doing this? He was out of town of course, leaving me to deal with repair men, carpet layers, electricians and general handy guys who now populated my house and were the only people I actually spoke to in the course of the day.

The phone clerk then dealt me the final blow, asking, "And what kind of extra line would you like for your modem?" I started to laugh hysterically. I knew I couldn't hang up on her. She was standing right in front of me. I was in the throes of re-entry shock.

Carlanne Herzog hits it right on the button when she explains that culture shock assails us in both mental and emotional ways.

"Mentally, we are required to cope daily with an incredible number of decisions. We had learned to function in a foreign culture in ways that differed from back home and this only serves to confuse and frustrate still more. Then, in the midst of re-educating ourselves our minds become overloaded. It is a real shock," she says.

Meditation for Dummies

In her blog, Carolyn Vines muses about meditation, shares her own story of a physical problem and inspires the reader to consider the practice of meditation too.

Carolyn is the winner of best international blog 2009
www.blackandabroad.com

Meditating is one of those practices we all know we should add to our daily/weekly regimes but rarely ever manage to incorporate. I've used every reason (read excuse) in the book for avoiding meditation: "I can't seem to find 10 minutes of quiet time", "I don't know how", "It's really something for gurus and the like". I don't know about you, but I find the idea of meditating quite intimidating, you know, twisting your body like a sitting pretzel and chanting "om" for hours on end. I recently (two days ago) found out that learning to meditate, at least in the beginning, doesn't involve making time or even making your body do almost inhuman things. This week's Living Smarter not Harder tip is to share a bit of wisdom passed along to me about quieting my mind.

Eleven years ago I was diagnosed with ulcerative colitis, a chronic condition affecting my large intestines. My GP explained that curing colitis is not possible and that I would have to take medicine for the rest of my life. From the very beginning I refused to accept this prognosis about my life and vowed to find a way to prove it wrong. After years of taking meds and somewhat following my doctors' advice to lower my stress level and reduce dairy products, which admittedly have helped to minimize my symptoms, I decided to try something different.

I went to the Internet and started looking for information on alternative medicine and stumbled across Ayurveda, an ancient, holistic Indian system of healing. The basic premise of Ayurveda is to achieve and maintain emotional, spiritual, and physical (lifestyle) balance. As each person is biologically different, it stands that any "disease" or disruption in balance, will manifest itself differently. On my first visit a little over a year ago, my vadya (I think this is what a practitioner of Ayurveda is called) said that he wasn't as interested in the colitis as what was going on in my life that allowed it to manifest. What followed was a year of continuing my efforts to heal the tragedies that beset my youth, getting accustomed to a slight change in my dietary habits, and finding ways to enjoy a healthier lifestyle (sleeping 7-8 hours, finding a fulfilling career at home, quality time with family, and so on).

On Sunday I was happy to report to my vadya that I've had no symptoms for about a year, and, best of all, my thinking has become clearer and more positive. However, I'm still struggling to quiet my mind. It's always going. That's when he told me, and not for the first time, that I needed to learn how to meditate.

"How do I do that?" I asked.

"By focusing 100% of your attention to whatever it is you're doing," he explained. According to his philosophy, by training my mind to block all thoughts that distract me from the task at hand, I'll eventually develop the skill to empty my mind while taking on "traditional" meditation.

"When you're eating," he began, "sit and eat. Look at the food on your plate, taking in its colors and form. Smell it. As you're chewing it, pay attention to how each morsel tastes. Turn off the TV; close your book or magazine; put the cell phone away and just eat." Meditation is a process, and if I apply this art of focused attention, I'm laying the foundation quieting my mind in meditation.

Eager to learn, I've put this art into practice the last two days. It's not easy, but when has learning ever been easy? To remind myself to keep at it, I've put "meditation" in my day planner as one of my top priorities everyday. Thank you, Dr. Mehta, for your wisdom and this week's tip.

The Day I Came Undone

Kim Brice, who was brought up in America and has a French father, wrote this story about an incident from her childhood when her younger brother refused to brush his teeth. This is filled with emotion and the characters of Marc and her parents are strong and vivid.

It started out like an average Saturday night in our house in Hampton Bays, a village tucked away on Long Island, the part that rich and famous New Yorkers use as their summer playground. Hampton Bays became home for us on the weekends. Marc, my older brother, and I had just taken a bath. We were standing in front of the brick fireplace perfectly nestled in a blood red living room wall. We were comfortably roasting our bodies like marshmallows in front of the fireplace, keeping warm as we waited for our favorite television program to start, Howard Cosell's Wide World of Sports. Marc was already quite a jock by then and to watch his heroes on TV was a life or death affair for him.

"I'm not brushing now," Marc said, his strong, ten year old compact body standing strong and firm. His moist chocolate brown hair was glistening in the light from the flames. Marc had decided he did not want to brush his teeth, at least not on command. My mother, Betty, asked him several times politely. My mother has always been patient and a soft soul. She hates raising her voice.

"Living with the French taught me to scream," she always says. "I had to learn to defend myself their way and I still hate it."

My mother pleaded with Marc but despite her insistence nothing more than Marc's refusals cascaded in. So she started raising her voice. Marc just resisted more and more. To this day, he has the persistence of a child, the kind that wears you down inside and out.

My father, Michel, was reading the New York Times, his favorite and almost only pastime. He peeped once or twice from behind the pages of his paper, showing that he was somehow connected to the goings on. My father is strong as a bull, physically and emotionally.

In the forty years he worked for his company, he probably called in sick once and that's because he couldn't walk because he had just had a hernia operation. He managed his life with the false illusion that everything could be controlled, his family, his work, his emotions. But he'd pour his heart out to perfect strangers.

"It's really a tragedy what's happening to your country and to your people. That's the way the world is, full of injustice," he said I don't know how many times to the Haitian man who sold him his newspaper at dawn every morning at the entrance to his subway stop on his way to work.

My mother finally lost it and the eventual screech in her voice sufficiently interrupted my father's concentration to make him decide to put his paper down and join into battle.

"Marc, you are GOING to brush your teeth and you HAVE NOTHING to say about it!" he commanded, spittle had already accumulated at the sides of his mouth.

Until then I just thought it had been the usual endless tit-for-tat but now I started getting anxious. My father was mad. Marc stood his ground.

It only took a few seconds before my father flung himself off the sofa and dove at my brother yelling, *"Espèce d'abruti!"* By this time, my brother's expression had turned from that of a cocky ten year old to a trapped little boy, totally unprepared for his predicament. He was physically overpowered and he knew it.

It didn't take long before they were in the bathroom battling it out. The veins in my father's neck were exploding with fury; one hand was squeezing my brother's arm and the other his neck. The unmerciful fluorescent lights were buzzing overhead, intensifying this wrestle of wills. Cry, spit and toothpaste were pouring down my brother's neck and chin. Marc's tears were not from fear or regret but audacity and his insatiable instinct for survival. After all, he had sustained much greater physical pain by that age and I knew he could handle it. Once he walked several miles home with a severed skull after his baseball mitt had gotten stuck in his bicycle wheel and sent him flying over his handlebars onto a gravel road.

I stood at the entrance of the bathroom scared and desperate. I had to save my brother.

"PAPA... STOP, PLEASE STOP! He didn't mean it." My screams scratched my throat and my tears begged for his mercy. I was of no consequence; it would have to end when it was over.

It did eventually end. We all survived. Marc didn't die but an emotional pain gnaws at his life unnoticed like undiagnosed cancer. My father continued to retreat like a turtle into a comfortable shell, alone with himself, in himself. My mother continues to outdo herself with the yelling. As for me, I have a recurring dream since that day. The scenarios are always different but there is a recurring theme. I'm desperate and panicking. I'm alone but I can feel there are people around me that I believe can save me. I scream out for help, endlessly. I have a voice but it doesn't project. It's strong inside but inaudible outside. I'm never heard. This scene just goes on and nothing ever happens. This dream started the day I became undone.

* "You moron!"

Extract – Taxi by Anika Smit

Thirteen-year-old South African, Anika Smit, tells the story of her trip to market with her family's home help when they were living in China.

Susan, Her Scooter and the Fish

On Fridays, Mom gave us cooking lessons. It was on one of those occasions where Susan, our *Ayee* (a Chinese word for somebody who helps to clean your house), got the idea of showing us how to make Chinese food too.

Susan owned her own restaurant before she started working at Zijin. One afternoon she invited me to go with her and put me on the back of her scooter. We rode down to the market to buy ingredients for the meal she would be making us later. That evening we were having Chinese and Western friends over for a celebration of David's birthday. We first stopped at her house so that I could meet her mother who lived with her. Susan lives in a real Chinese courtyard, in a two-storied house with a washing machine. Her mother is very friendly - a real old Chinese woman. Susan is very protective towards me. She gave everyone a dirty look that even dared to look into my direction.

I had no clue what I was in for, and maybe it was better that way. This was my first visit to the market in Zhong Shan Ling. To tell the honest truth, I did not even know that there was a market there. Susan grabbed me by the arm and in we went to the indoor meat market. Before I had a chance to look around, I was standing in front of a bloody fish tank. My stomach made the biggest turn it had ever made. It was one of those 'you've gotta be kidding' moments you grow accustomed to in China.

Susan bought a huge fish, and caught it on her own. I am sure it was one of the biggest fish I had ever seen. And it was still very much alive too! The shopkeeper asked if he should kill the fish. Susan said, "No!" So he put the fish in a clear plastic bag which Susan gave me to carry. The fish flapped around and its mouth opened and closed for air; it hurt my feelings to see an animal suffer like that. She bought a collection of other ingredients too before we returned.

By this time, my leg was red from the live fish slapping against it. Susan put me on the back of the scooter again, with the fish between us. It was still flopping around! It got so bad that it even fell off the scooter, out of the bag and into the mud. Susan told me to get off the scooter and put it back into the bag again.

What skills do I need to use to catch a fish that is out of the water, fighting for its life? Do you need one or two hands, or do you need to step on it with your foot? The outdoor toilet had a smell that blew your breath away. Why the fish decided to jump out right at that spot, I don't know. As if matters weren't bad enough, the puddle was filled with fresh 'natural fertilizer' that was being used on the farm next door. Using one foot and two hands was the way to do it!

After the highly disturbing scooter ride up the mountain, we finally reached home. Susan asked me to go and fill the bathtub with water. The half-dead fish regained a little bit of consciousness in Mom's bathtub. Minutes later, Susan took the flapping fish and threw it into the kitchen sink – with the dishes still in it! She asked me to take the dishes out, and just when

I got hold of them, the fish threw up a wave of bloody water. I started screaming! Susan grabbed the fish by the tail and started slamming it against the kitchen counter. The fish's eyeballs fell out and blood splattered everywhere – into the coffee, into the sugar and into Mom's already prepared Western food. Susan scaled the fish alive with her long fingernails. The Chinese, even the men, believe that they should grow their fingernails because it is a sign that they don't need to work so hard to make a living. The poor fish died slowly but surely – with Susan stabbing it furiously with a large kitchen knife. She cooked the fish up into a very spicy stew.

Everybody enjoyed the fish very much that evening – it was a local delicacy. Mom was very thankful for Susan's cooking because her food was not enough. I was also very happy because now I know never to cook Chinese fish!

Your task

Take a story from the list you made earlier and write about it now. Write a story of 500-1000 words using the **seven steps for writing life story** and adding **SPICE**.

Seven steps to writing life stories

1. Compose
2. Review
3. Draft
4. Review
5. Polish
6. Revisit
7. Save

Spice up your life stories

- **S**pecifics
- **P**lace
- **I**ncident
- **C**haracter
- **E**motion

If you are taking the Personal Feedback Program

Please save and name your completed exercise using the YOURNAMEEIGHT naming convention and email it to feedback@joparfitt.com

Within two weeks you will receive feedback for this **Lesson Eight**. In the meantime, while you are waiting, please enjoy your **Bonus Lesson - The editing process, the Just Write inspirational stickers** and the **Getting Inspired** sections that follow.

I hope you have enjoyed this course and that your memories are now on the page rather than simply in your head. Now you are ready to share your stories with other people. Thank you for letting me be part of your journey.

With best wishes

Happy writing

Jo Parfitt

BONUS LESSON

The editing process

One of the best ways for you to be able to edit and polish your work is to learn by the mistakes of others. I have been teaching for many years and find that students make similar mistakes. The list below will help you to spot these mistakes in your own writing. Take a look.

The twenty most common mistakes

1. **Telling** rather than **showing**. Did you really show what people were doing? Did you say 'he was angry'? That's **telling**. Or did you say 'he slammed the door so hard it shook in its frame.' That's **showing**.

2. **Forgetting specifics.** If you are French, for example, you need to call your father 'Papa' not 'Dad', unless of course, you called him 'Dad'. Use the words you used for people's names as this adds atmosphere and authenticity.

3. **Too many dashes and brackets.** If you have too many dashes – like this – it can look a bit messy on the page. Similarly too many brackets (like adding this, for example) can make your sentences overlong and with too many subclauses. Often you can cut the dashes and brackets and replace them with commas or split the sentence in two, using a full stop.

4. **Too many exclamation marks!** It is easy to use exclamation marks to indicate where you said something surprising or you shouted. Or to flag a funny moment. The more !!! you have the less impact they have on the reader and become invisible. Try to keep them to a maximum of one per page.

5. **Unclear use of foreign words.** Use foreign words for sure, to add atmosphere, authenticity and detail. Words for relatives, such as Mama, Papa and Opa or Boulevard Montparnasse do not need to be in italics because they are considered to be names. But other words that may not be understood need to be in italics. Words not in common parlance need to be explained in a subtle way just in case the reader does not understand. Latin words like ad hoc do not need explanation.

6. **Mixed tenses.** Try to keep the whole piece in the past tense or present tense. Often you can start off in one tense but slip into another.

7. **Consistency and thoughts.** You do not need to put thoughts in inverted commas. "Gosh, it's hot," I thought. However, you can do so if you like. Whatever you decide to do, you need to be consistent.

8. **Missed opportunities for dialogue.** Each time you tell a story, you can, of course just **tell** the story: Jane was hungry so she went to look in the fridge. But you could also turn it into a piece of dialogue with movement: "I'm so hungry I could commit murder," Jane growled, rubbing her stomach and scanning the unfamiliar kitchen for something resembling a

fridge. "Come on. Come on, I know you are in there somewhere," she continued opening one sleek white cupboard door after another.

9. **Not adding action to dialogue.** If you show us what the person did while he was speaking or after he spoke it makes the dialogue more interesting and provides an opportunity to show the character of the speaker. As in the example with Jane, above, we can see she is impatient and in a bad temper by the actions she makes.

10. **Inaccurate dialogue layout.** It is very common for students to put the inverted commas and final comma or full stop the wrong way round in a piece of dialogue. Let me show you:

   a. "Hello", said Jane is wrong.

   b. "Hello," said Jane is right.

11. **Dialogue that does not start on a new line.** Dialogue, or the piece containing dialogue, should always start a new line. Each time a new person speaks, you move to a new line.

12. **Repeating words.** Try not to use the same word twice in the same sentence or in consecutive sentences.

13. **Lack of detail.** Try to name the tree, the flower, the bird, rather than saying: 'the bird landed on the branch of the tree' but: 'The robin landed on the branch of the willow'. If you write: 'the view was incredible' that does not paint a picture. I cannot see it. Help the reader to see what you saw.

14. **Empty words.** Using 'really', 'truly', 'literally' and other similar words does not generally lend anything to the text. 'A really long road' is still long, even if you write: 'a long road'.

15. **Clichés.** Try to avoid them.

16. **Mum or mum?** This is such a common mistake, I can't tell you. When mum is used like a name, it has a capital: "Can you help me, Mum?" or 'Mum walked into the room.' But when you are writing generically about mums or mothers they do not need a capital: 'My mum is always in a bad mood,' or 'I hate the way mothers are always cross,' but 'Mum is always in a bad mood,' or 'I hate the way Mother is always cross.'

17. **Lack of emotion.** If you want your piece to be authentic it is important that you show how the people you write about feel.

18. **Complicated writing.** They say that if you want your writing to be accessible you should write at the level of a 13 year old. Try to keep your writing simple, if you can, choosing short words over long. The way to tell if your writing is complicated is to read it aloud. If you find yourself stumbling when you read it, it needs simplifying.

19. **Overlong sentences.** Short sentences give a piece pace. As a rule, if your sentence is four lines long or more it is too long. If you read it aloud you will run out of breath. Try to split long sentences up if you can.

20. **Characters without identity.** When you use a name it conjures up a picture of the person. To say that 'a man helped me to find my lost purse' does not allow us to see the man in any way. Give him a name and it helps us to see him and, importantly to remember who

he is. If you do not know his name, then find a way to describe him. Perhaps he is a tramp or carries an umbrella or wears sandals. Give him an identity.

The editing process

If you choose to take this program with personal feedback then you will receive a critique for your first draft of all your lessons. This student, Jenny, chose to follow the **Gold**, Extended, option, paying an additional £30 to polish this piece about her father.

If you are not taking the personal feedback or extended options, then please work with a friend or editor, who can guide you through the polishing process.

Join me now as we follow a piece of Jenny's work as it moves through the editing process. This piece doubled in length to almost 800 words by the time we had worked on it thoroughly. Take a look at my comments (in the boxes in the right hand margin) and notice the changes I made to the text (highlighted in grey).

STEP ONE - First Draft

This is how Jenny's homework arrived on my desk:

LESSON ONE - VERSION ONE

I looked out of the window today and noticed the blossom forming on my winter flowering prunus tree. It took me back to the time twenty years ago when we bought this house. The garden was totally bare so I had a free rein, so made a mental note of all the trees and shrubs which I like the most, not to mention flowers, which would come later.

As I didn't know where to start when the time came to plant up the garden, which is not particularly large and has a stone wall around it, I looked in the local paper for a garden plant supplier. Sure enough there was an advertisement for a firm called "Paint it and Plant it".

"Sounds reasonable," I thought , especially as the planting bit would have defeated me. When it comes to gardening, my husband is as useful as a bucket full of holes. A local plumber once said to me, "I wouldn't even trust your husband with a bucket full of water." He had a point.

Along came Mr Plantit and he discussed the required number of trees and shrubs to fill the space, leaving room for a lawn on which my grandchildren (not that I had any at that time, mind you) and dog could play, of course. Mr Plantit arrived some time later with a lorry loaded with the chosen items, all very small and insignificant.

"Don't you worry, madam, give it a few years and it will be lovely," Mr Plantit assured me. Twenty years on the garden resembles a jungle unless we continually prune, lop, cut back or chop down. Nevertheless, we have lots of colour, shade and interest, so our cottage garden continues to delight. Yes, Mr Plantit was over-enthusiastic in his recommendations, but for the most part he got it right. We chose trees of differing colours, a red rhus, yellow maple and a weeping cherry that flowers in the spring and which was really popular with my grandchildren because its branches reached the ground and they could hide amongst them or make a house within. The large cotinus turns to burnished gold in the autumn and smothers my greenhouse roof with leaves, or shades it from hot sun in the height of summer.

Alas when it reached its teens, the weeping cherry became unruly, waving its gangly branches to the sky and had to be knocked into shape. We were forced to turn it from an upturned bowl into a kind of toadstool with a skinny stem shape because it got so unruly. Fortunately, by then the grandchildren, who had all arrived, four of them, had outgrown it long ago.

STEP TWO - First Draft critiqued

Here are my initial comments:

LESSON ONE - EDITED

I looked out of the window today and noticed the blossom forming on my winter flowering prunus tree. It took me back to the time twenty years ago when we bought this house. The garden was totally bare so I had a free rein, so made a mental note of all the trees and shrubs which I like the most, not to mention flowers, which would come later.

As I didn't know where to start when the time came to plant up the garden, which is not particularly large and has a stone wall around it, I looked in the local paper for a garden plant supplier. Sure enough there was an advertisement for a firm called "Paint it and Plant it".

"Sounds reasonable," I thought , especially as the planting bit would have defeated me. When it comes to gardening, my husband is as useful as a bucket full of holes. A local plumber once said to me, "I wouldn't even trust your husband with a bucket full of water." He had a point.

Along came Mr Plantit and he discussed the required number of trees and shrubs to fill the space, leaving room for a lawn on which my grandchildren (not that I had any at that time, mind you) and dog could play, of course. Mr Plantit arrived some time later with a lorry loaded with the chosen items, all very small and insignificant.

"Don't you worry, madam, give it a few years and it will be lovely," Mr Plantit assured me.

Twenty years on the garden resembles a jungle unless we continually prune, lop, cut back or chop down. Nevertheless, we have lots of colour, shade and interest, so our cottage garden continues to delight. Yes, Mr Plantit was over-enthusiastic in his recommendations, but for the most part he got it right. We chose trees of differing colours, a red rhus, yellow maple and a weeping cherry that flowers in the spring and which was really popular with my grandchildren because its branches reached the ground and they could hide amongst them or make a house within. The large cotinus turns to burnished gold in the autumn and smothers my greenhouse roof with leaves, or shades it from hot sun in the height of summer.

Alas when it reached its teens, the weeping cherry became unruly, waving its gangly branches to the sky and had to be knocked into shape. We were forced to turn it from an upturned bowl into a kind of toadstool with a skinny stem shape because it got so unruly. Fortunately, by then the grandchildren, who had all arrived, four of them, had outgrown it long ago.

STEP THREE - Second Draft

And this is how Jenny made improvements:

LESSON ONE - SECOND DRAFT

I looked out of the window today and noticed the blossom forming on my winter flowering prunus tree. It took me back to the time twenty years ago when we bought this house. The garden was totally bare so I had a free rein and made a mental note of all the trees and shrubs which I like the most, not to mention flowers, which would come later Our house is a converted stable block and the garden was once a crewyard; the builder had simply turfed the whole area but this didn't suit me. I had spent many happy hours as a younger person helping my father in our wonderful country garden . I must have inherited his desire to create beautiful surroundings, and let's face it, I am a bit of an artist! As I didn't know where to start when the time came to plant up the garden which is not particularly large and has a honey coloured stone wall around it, I looked in the local paper for a garden plant supplier. Sure enough there was an advertisement for a firm called "Paint it and Plant it".

"Sounds reasonable" I thought , especially as the planting bit would have defeated me. When it comes to gardening, my husband is as useful as a bucket full of holes. A local plumber once said to me "I wouldn't even trust your husband with a bucket full of water." He had a point.

Along came Mr Plantit which of course wasn't his name, but he was a delightful man, tall, thin and dressed in country tweeds, and he discussed the required number of trees and shrubs to fill the space, leaving room for a lawn on which any future grandchildren and our dog could play, of course. Mr Plantit arrived some time later with a lorry loaded with the chosen items, all very small and insignificant. "That will never fill the space" I muttered.

"Don't you worry, madam, give it a few years and it will be lovely," Mr Plantit assured me. He set to work happily digging holes, still unsuitably dressed but perfectly content with the huge task I had set him.

Twenty years on the garden resembles a jungle unless we continually prune, lop, chop or cut back . . Nevertheless, we have lots of colour, shade and interest, so our cottage garden continues t o delight. Yes, Mr Plantit was over enthusiastic in his recommendations, because everything grew so huge, but for the most part he got it right. We chose trees of differing colours, a red rhus, yellow maple and a weeping cherry which flowers in the spring and which was really popular with my grandchildren because its branches reached the ground and they could hide amongst them or make a house inside. The large cotinus turns to burnished gold in the autumn and smothers my greenhouse roof with leaves, or shades it from hot sun in the height of summer.

Alas, as it reached its teens, the weeping cherry became unruly, waving its gangly branches to the sky and so had to be pruned into shape. We were forced to turn our lovely pink and green cascade into a kind of toadstool with a skinny stem. Fortunately by then the grandchildren, all four of them, had outgrown it a few years back.

STEP FOUR - Second Draft is critiqued

The piece is vastly improved, but I still have more comments, mostly because, though Jenny did attempt to follow all my suggestions, I felt she needed to expand still further.

LESSON ONE – SECOND DRAFT

I looked out of the window today and noticed the blossom forming on my winter flowering prunus tree. It took me back to the time twenty years ago when we bought this house. The garden was totally bare when we moved in, so I had a free rein to create my own garden from scratch. I made a mental note of all the trees and shrubs that I like the most, not to mention flowers, which would come later . Our house is a converted stable block and the garden was once a crewyard; the builder had simply turfed the whole area but this didn't suit me. I had spent many happy hours as a younger person helping my father in our wonderful country garden . I must have inherited his desire to create beautiful surroundings, and let's face it, I am a bit of an artist!

As I didn't know where to start when the time came to plant up the garden, which is not particularly large and has a honey coloured stone wall around it, I looked in the local paper for a garden plant supplier. Sure enough there was an advertisement for a firm called "Paint it and Plant it".

"Sounds reasonable," I thought , especially as the planting bit would have defeated me. When it comes to gardening, my husband is as useful as a bucket full of holes. A local plumber once said to me, "I wouldn't even trust your husband with a bucket full of water." He had a point.

Along came Mr Plantit, which of course wasn't his name, but he was a delightful man, tall, thin and dressed in country tweeds, and he discussed the required number of trees and shrubs to fill the space, leaving room for a lawn on which any future grandchildren and our dog could play, of course. Mr Plantit returned some time later with a lorry loaded with the chosen items, all very small and insignificant. "That will never fill the space," I muttered.

"Don't you worry, madam," he assured me. "Give it a few years and it will be lovely." He set to work happily digging holes, still unsuitably dressed but perfectly content with the huge task I had set him.

Twenty years on the garden resembles a jungle unless we continually prune, lop, chop or cut back. Nevertheless, we have lots of colour, shade and interest, so our cottage garden continues to delight. Yes, Mr Plantit was over enthusiastic in his recommendations, because everything grew so huge, but for the most part he got it right. We chose trees of differing colours, a red rhus, yellow maple and a weeping cherry, which flowers in the spring and that was really popular with my grandchildren because its branches reached the ground and they could hide amongst them or make a house inside. The large cotinus turns to burnished gold in the autumn and smothers my greenhouse roof with leaves, or shades it from hot sun in the height of summer.

Sadly, as it reached its teens, the weeping cherry became unruly, waving its gangly branches to the sky and so had to be pruned into shape. We were forced to turn our lovely pink and green cascade into a kind of toadstool with a skinny stem. Fortunately by then the grandchildren, all four of them, had outgrown it.

Jo Parfitt 11/25/09 7:14 PM
Comment: Tell me more about this. You say 'younger person' but give us a clue. I know you mean Garden Cottage, but the reader doesn't. Show me how your father, in his tweed jacket would be bent over a rose bush or something, pruning away, happy as a lark. Or how he measured a day's garden success in bags of rubbish!

Jo Parfitt 11/25/09 7:14 PM
Comment: This is much better. Much. I'm just telling you how to make it even better still. I want to see Grandpa.

Jo Parfitt 11/25/09 7:14 PM
Comment: How large? Your 'not particularly' may not be my 'not particularly'. A Dutch person would call your garden huge and an American may consider it small! It is the size of a tennis court and a half, maybe? A tennis court? Twice the footprint of the house? The garden goes along one side of the house.

Jo Parfitt 11/25/09 7:14 PM
Comment: Although you do not need to put thoughts in quotes, if you do, you need to put a comma before the final inverted comma. Also, when you precede a piece of dialogue, like here, with 'the plumber said to me' you need a comma or a colon then a space then the opening inverted comma. I used a comma.

Jo Parfitt 12/2/09 1:08 PM
Comment: Please can you add some of the names of the plants here?

Jo Parfitt 11/25/09 7:14 PM
Comment: This would be a nice place to split the dialogue,

Jo Parfitt 11/25/09 7:14 PM
Comment: You have a comma before a which but not before a that.

Jo Parfitt 12/2/09 1:09 PM
Comment: Alas is a bit old-fashioned. I changed it to 'sadly'

Jo Parfitt 11/25/09 7:14 PM
Comment: The ending is more dramatic to end after the it.

STEP FIVE - Third Draft

And this is how Jenny made improvements:

I looked out of the window today and noticed the blossom forming on my winter flowering prunus tree. It took me back to the time twenty years ago when we bought this house. The garden was totally bare when we moved in, so I had a free rein to create my own garden from scratch. I made a mental note of all the trees and shrubs that I like the most, not to mention flowers, which would come later . Our house is a converted stable block and the garden was once a crewyard; the builder had simply turfed the whole area but this didn't suit me. I had spent many happy hours as a teenager still living at home helping my father in our wonderful country garden, which was so large that it had an orchard of apple trees and a vegetable plot. When my father wasn't at work he spent every waking hour tending his plants and I was always happy to help him. I must have inherited his desire to create beautiful surroundings, and let's face it, I am a bit of an artist.

As I didn't know where to start when the time came to plant up the garden, which is not much larger than a tennis court and has a honey coloured stone wall on three sides, I looked in the local paper for a garden plant supplier. Sure enough there was an advertisement for a firm called "Paint it and Plant it".

Sounds reasonable, I thought, especially as the planting bit would have defeated me. When it comes to gardening, my husband is as useful as a bucket full of holes. A local plumber once said to me, "I wouldn't even trust your husband with a bucket full of water." He had a point. Along came Mr Plantit, which of course wasn't his name, but he was a delightful man, tall, thin and dressed in country tweeds, and he discussed the required number of trees and shrubs to fill the space, leaving room for a lawn on which any future grandchildren and our dog could play, of course. Mr Plantit returned some time later with a lorry loaded with the chosen items, both trees and shrubs all very small and insignificant. The shrubs I particularly wanted were mostly brightly coloured and some had variegated leaves while some were spring flowering."That will never fill the space," I muttered.

"Don't you worry, madam," he assured me. "Give it a few years and it will be lovely." He set to work happily digging holes, still unsuitably dressed but perfectly content with the huge task I had set him.

Twenty years on the garden resembles a jungle unless we continually prune, lop, chop or cut back. Nevertheless, we have lots of colour, shade and interest, so our cottage garden continues to delight. Yes, Mr Plantit was over enthusiastic in his recommendations, because everything grew so huge, but for the most part he got it right. We chose trees of differing colours, a red rhus, yellow maple and a weeping cherry, which flowers in the spring and that was really popular with my grandchildren because its branches reached the ground and they could hide amongst them or make a house inside. The large cotinus turns to burnished gold in the autumn and smothers my greenhouse roof with leaves, or shades it from hot sun in the height of summer.

Sadly, as it reached its teens, the weeping cherry became unruly, waving its gangly branches to the sky and so had to be pruned into shape. We were forced to turn our lovely pink and green cascade into a kind of toadstool with a skinny stem. Fortunately by then the grandchildren, all four of them, had outgrown it.

I often wonder what my dear old dad would think of my cottage garden. Hope he would be proud of me.

STEP SIX - Third Draft is critiqued

The piece is now almost perfect. See how I just made a few changes and suggestions:

LESSON ONE – THIRD DRAFT

I looked out of the window today and noticed the blossom forming on my winter flowering prunus tree. It took me back to the time twenty years ago when we bought this house. The garden was totally bare when we moved in, so I had a free rein to create my own garden from scratch. I made a mental note of all the trees and shrubs that I like the most, not to mention flowers, which would come later . Our house is a converted stable block and the garden was once a crewyard; the builder had simply turfed the whole area but this didn't suit me. I had spent many happy hours as a teenager still living at home helping my father in our wonderful country garden, which was so large that it had an orchard of apple trees and a vegetable plot. When my father wasn't at work he spent every waking hour bent over his plants and I was always happy to help him. I must have inherited his desire to create beautiful surroundings, and let's face it, I am a bit of an artist.

> **Jo Parfitt** 11/27/09 11:03 AM
> **Comment:** Bent over lets me see him better.

As I didn't know where to start when the time came to plant up the garden, which is not much larger than a tennis court and has a honey coloured stone wall on three sides, I looked in the local paper for a garden plant supplier. Sure enough there was an advertisement for a firm called "Paint it and Plant it".

Sounds reasonable, I thought, especially as the planting bit would have defeated me. When it comes to gardening, my husband is as useful as a bucket full of holes. A local plumber once said to me, "I wouldn't even trust your husband with a bucket full of water." He had a point.

> **Jo Parfitt** 11/27/09 11:03 AM
> **Comment:** I removed the " round your thoughts.

> **Jo Parfitt** 11/27/09 11:03 AM
> **Comment:** I don't think you need a 'but' here and 2 sentences may be better.

Along came Mr Plantit, which of course wasn't his name. He was a delightful man, tall, thin and dressed in country tweeds. We discussed the required number of trees and shrubs to fill the space, leaving room for a lawn on which any future grandchildren and our dog could play, of course. Mr Plantit returned some time later with a lorry loaded with the chosen items, both trees and shrubs all very small and insignificant. The shrubs I particularly wanted were mostly brightly coloured and some had variegated leaves while some were spring flowering. I knew what I wanted. Year round colour. "Huh! That will never fill the space," I muttered under my breath.. I hadn't counted on quite that many gaps.

> **Jo Parfitt** 11/27/09 11:03 AM
> **Comment:** Now I split the sentence up because it was a bit long

> **Jo Parfitt** 11/27/09 11:03 AM
> **Comment:** Adding 'Huh!' and 'under my breath' shows more of your emotion

"Don't you worry, madam," he assured me. "Give it a few years and it will be lovely." He set to work happily digging holes, still unsuitably dressed but perfectly content with the huge task I had set him.

Twenty years on the garden resembles a jungle unless we continually prune, lop, chop or cut back. Nevertheless, we have lots of colour, shade and interest, so our cottage garden continues to delight. In the end, Mr Plantit had been over enthusiastic in his recommendations, because everything grew so huge, but for the most part he got it right. We are glad we chose trees of differing colours – a red rhus, yellow maple and a weeping cherry that flowers in the spring and was really popular with my grandchildren. It had not taken long for its branches to reach the ground and Sam, Josh, Phoebe and Ben could hide behind them or make a house inside. The large cotinus turns to burnished gold in the autumn and smothers my greenhouse roof with leaves, or shades it from hot sun in the height of summer.

Sadly, as it reached its teens, the weeping cherry became unruly, waving its gangly branches to the sky and so had to be pruned into shape. We were forced to turn our lovely pink and green cascade into a kind of toadstool with a skinny stem. Fortunately by then the grandchildren, all four of them, had outgrown it.

I often wonder what my dear old dad would think of my cottage garden and hope he would be proud of me.

Now, there is no more to do! Jenny is finished!

LESSON ONE – FOURTH DRAFT

I looked out of the window today and noticed the blossom forming on my winter flowering prunus tree. It took me back to the time twenty years ago when we bought this house. The garden was totally bare when we moved in, so I had a free rein to create my own garden from scratch. I made a mental note of all the trees and shrubs that I like the most, not to mention flowers, which would come later . Our house is a converted stable block and the garden was once a crewyard; the builder had simply turfed the whole area but this didn't suit me. I had spent many happy hours as a teenager still living at home helping my father, a widower, in our wonderful country garden, which was so large that it had an orchard of apple and pear trees and a vegetable plot. When my father wasn't at work he spent every waking hour bent over his plants and I was always happy to help him. He was a tall, skinny quietly spoken man who smoked constantly whatever he was doing, and I remember he had a drip on the end of his nose when gardening in cold weather. His flat cap and muffler were as essential as his cigarettes. However, I must have inherited his desire to create beautiful surroundings, and let's face it, I am a bit of an artist.

As I didn't know where to start when the time came to plant up the garden, which is not much larger than a tennis court and has a honey coloured stone wall on three sides, I looked in the local paper for a garden plant supplier. Sure enough there was an advertisement for a firm called "Paint it and Plant it".

Sounds reasonable, I thought, especially as the planting bit would have defeated me. When it comes to gardening, my husband is as useful as a bucket full of holes. A local plumber once said to me, "I wouldn't even trust your husband with a bucket full of water." He had a point.

Along came Mr Plantit, which of course wasn't his name. He was a delightful man, tall, thin and dressed in country tweeds. We discussed the required number of trees and shrubs to fill the space, leaving room for a lawn on which any future grandchildren and our dog could play, of course. Mr Plantit returned some time later with a lorry loaded with the chosen items, both trees and shrubs all very small and insignificant. The shrubs I particularly wanted were mostly brightly coloured and some had variegated leaves while some were spring flowering. I knew what I wanted. Year round colour. "Huh! That will never fill the space," I muttered under my breath.. I hadn't counted on quite that many gaps.

"Don't you worry, madam," he assured me. "Give it a few years and it will be lovely." He set to work happily digging holes, still unsuitably dressed but perfectly content with the huge task I had set him.

Twenty years on the garden resembles a jungle unless we continually prune, lop, chop or cut back. Nevertheless, we have lots of colour, shade and interest, so our cottage garden continues to delight. In the end, Mr Plantit had been over enthusiastic in his recommendations, because everything grew so huge, but for the most part he got it right. We are glad we chose trees of differing colours – a red rhus, yellow maple and a weeping cherry that flowers in the spring and was really popular with my grandchildren. It had not taken long for its branches to reach the ground and Sam, Josh, Phoebe and Ben could hide behind them or make a house inside. The large cotinus turns to burnished gold in the autumn and smothers my greenhouse roof with leaves, or shades it from hot sun in the height of summer.

Sadly, as it reached its teens, the weeping cherry became unruly, waving its gangly branches to the sky and so had to be pruned into shape. We were forced to turn our lovely pink and green cascade into a kind of toadstool with a skinny stem. Fortunately by then the grandchildren, all four of them, had outgrown it.

I often wonder what my dear old dad would think of my cottage garden and hope he would be proud of me.

Getting inspired

Be inspired by others who have published life story by reading the following:

- Autobiographies
- Blogs
- Columns
- Memoirs
- Journals
- Non-fiction based on the author's own life experience

Here are some of my favourites:

Autobiographies

- A Moveable Feast – Ernest Hemingway
- Me Talk Pretty One Day - David Sedaris
- When You are Engulfed in Flames – David Sedaris
- Baggage - Janet Street-Porter
- The Great Failure – Natalie Goldberg
- Don't Tell Mum I Work on the Rigs, she thinks I am a piano player in a whorehouse – Paul Carter
- The Color of Water – James McBride
- Sound Bites – Alex Kapranos
- Julie and Julia – Julie White
- Petite Anglaise – Catherine Sanderson
- It's all Greek to Me –John Mole
- A Year in Provence – Peter Mayle
- Down and Out in Paris and London – George Orwell
- A Moveable Marriage – Robin Pascoe
- A Broad Abroad – Robin Pascoe
- Global Mom – Melissa Dalton Bradford
- Lunch in Paris – Elizabeth Bard
- Arrivals, Departures and the Adventures In-Between – Christoper O'Shaughnessy
- Harvesting Stones – Paula Lucas

Anthologies

- Tales from the Expat Harem – edited by Anastasia Ashman and Jennifer Gokmen at Seal Press
- The Sourcebook – The Expatriate Archive Centre
- Drinking Camel's Milk in the Yurt – Monica Neboli
- Knocked-Up Abroad – Lisa Ferland

To inspire writing

- Bird by Bird – Anne Lamott
- Writing in a New Convertible with the Top Down – Sheila Bender and Christi Killien
- On Writing – Stephen King
- The Treehouse – Naomi Wolff
- Old Friend From Far Away – Natalie Goldberg
- Writing Down the Bones – Natalie Goldberg
- The Artist's Way – Julia Cameron
- Writing to Save your Life – Michele Weldon
- Writing From Life –Susan Wittig Albert
- Writing Personal Essays – Sheila Bender

In this program

Books

- Letters Never Sent – Ruth van Reken
- Planet Germany – Cathy Dobson
- Forced to Fly – edited by Jo Parfitt
- A Moving Landscape – Jo Parfitt
- Postcards from Across the Pond – Mike Harling
- To the Manor Drawn – Leslie-Ann Bosher
- Planter's Tales – Mahbob Abdullah
- Should I Stay or Should I Go? – Paul Allen
- Black and Abroad – Carolyn Vines
- Homeward Bound – Robin Pascoe
- Tales from the Expat Harem – Anastasia Ashman and Jennifer Eaton Gokmen
- How to be a Global Grandparent – Peter Gosling and Anne Huscroft
- Taxi – Anika Smit
- Writing in a New Convertible with the Top Down – Sheila Bender and Christi Killien
- When You Are Engulfed in Flames – David Sedaris
- A Moveable Feast – Ernest Hemingway
- The Singing Warrior – Niamh Ni Bhroin

Just Write
inspirational stickers

If you would like to keep on writing and would benefit from having your memory jogged, then you are **encouraged to use the** Just Write inspirational stickers. They are designed in label format so that you can select one easily, stick it into your notebook and use it as the inspiration for a story. Alternatively you can also simply choose a subject and write directly onto your computer.

THANK YOU!

I hope you have enjoyed this Write Your Life Stories home study program as much as I enjoyed writing it.

If you would like any additional personal feedback please email me at feedback@joparfitt.com

If you would like to work with us to turn your stories into a book then please get in touch via jo@joparfitt.com

If you would like to share some of your edited stories with us in written or audio form and see them appear on our website for other students to enjoy, then please send them to us at jo@joparfitt.com

Happy writing

Jo Parfitt